MORALITY PLAY
Case Studies in Ethics

MORALITY PLAY
Case Studies in Ethics

Jessica Pierce

University of Colorado at Boulder

Boston   Burr Ridge, IL   Dubuque, IA   Madison, WI   New York
San Francisco   St. Louis   Bangkok   Bogotá   Caracas   Kuala Lumpur
Lisbon   London   Madrid   Mexico City   Milan   Montreal   New Delhi
Santiago   Seoul   Singapore   Sydney   Taipei   Toronto

 **Higher Education**

Morality Play: Case Studies in Ethics

2 3 4 5 6 7 8 9 0 DOC/DOC 0 9 8 7 6 5 4

ISBN 0-07-301120-7

Vice president and Editor-in-chief: *Emily Barrosse*
Publisher: *Lyn Uhl*
Sponsoring editor/Development editor: *Jon-David Hague*
Editorial assistant: *Allison Rona*
Marketing manager: *Zina Craft*
Project manager: *Mel Valentin*
Production supervisor: *Jason Huls*
Design manager: *Cassandra Chu*
Cover designer: *Joan Greenfield*
Interior designer: *Susan Breitbard*
Compositor: *International Typesetting and Composition*
Typeface: *10.5/12 Palatino*
Printer: *R. R. Donnelley/Crawfordsville*

Library of Congress Cataloging-in-Publication Data

Pierce, Jessica, 1965–
    Morality play : case studies in ethics / Jessica Pierce.
        p.   cm.
    Includes bibliographical references.
    ISBN 0-07-301120-7 (softcover)
    1. Ethics—Textbooks. 2. Ethics—Case studies. I. Title.

BJ1025.P54 2004
170—dc22   2004057939

http://www.mhhe.com

Table of Contents

Introduction   1

Chapter I   ## Crime and Punishment   13

Stanley "Tookie" Williams and the Problem of Redemption   14
The Execution of Scott Hain, Juvenile Offender   15
Bible Used in Conviction   18
Chemical Castration for Male Sex Offenders   20
Vicarious Sensitization   22
Torture of a Kidnapper   24
Three Nuns and a Silo   26
Stealing from the Wishing Well   28
The Consenting Victim   29
Execution of an Abortion-Provider's Killer   31
White-Collar Crime   32
White-Collar Crime, Take Two: Atlantic States Foundry   34

Chapter II   ## Life and Death   37

Elder Suicide or Dignified Exit? A Letter from Ohio   38
Fetal Rights and the Fetus as Person: The Case of J.D.S.   40
Fetal Rights, Take Two: Unborn Victims of Violence Act   41
Fetal Rights, Take Three: Drug Abuse and Fetal Abuse   42
Zero Population Growth   44
Suicide Concert   47

Growth Hormones for Shortness   48
Age-Based Cost Studies   51
Medical Care for Prisoners   53
Medical Care for Prisoners, Take Two: Donor Heart
    Goes to a Criminal   53
Medical Care for Prisoners, Take Three: Organ Transplant
    for Death Row Inmate   54
Fetal Testing for Down Syndrome   57
Age-Extension Research   60
The Schiavos   64

Chapter III   *Habitat and Humanity*   *67*

Troublesome Trinkets   68
Famine in Ethiopia   70
'A Hunting We Will Go . . .   74
Glofish   75
Ecoterrorism: Kill the Hummers!   77
War Is Terrorism   81
Dolphin Parks   81
Eating Sea Turtles   85
PBDE and the Precautionary Principle   88
Canned Hunts   92
Cosmetic Surgery for Pets   94
O Canada, How Could You?   97

Chapter IV   *Liberty and Coercion*   *101*

DanceSafe: Making Ecstasy Safer for Partyers   102
Banning Ephedra   104
Obesity: Personal or Political?   108
Worried about Harry Potter   112
Wal-Mart Keeps Its Shelves Clean   114

Edward "NJ Weedman" Forchion: Ganja Brings Him
    Closer to God   117
License-Plate Liberties   120
Pledge of Allegiance   120
Ed Rosenthal and Medical Marijuana   123
Cameras Watching Students   125
High School Tells Student to Remove Anti-War Shirt   127
CRACK—Get Sterilized, Get Cash   129
My Hummer, My Choice   132
"Let those Who Ride Decide": Motorcycle Helmet Laws and
    Biker Rights   133
USA Patriot Act   135

Chapter V   *Value and Culture*   *139*

Same-Sex Unions and the Defense of Marriage   140
Gay Sex and Adultery   144
Sex Education in School   145
Evolution vs. Creationism in Public Schools   147
Creationism, Take Two: Professor Dini's Recommendation   151
Sports Supplementation: Fair or Foul?   153
Sports Supplementation, Take Two: Ross Rebagliati   157
Extreme Makeover   158
Culture Wars   160
Bright Rights   163
A Call to Civil Society   165
Ethics for the Information Age: The SCANS Report   166
Character Education of Children   168
Character Education, Take Two: Georgia's
    "Respect for the Creator" Principle   173
Rigoberta Menchú: The Purpose of Truth   174

Topical Table of Contents

If you are interested in cases that deal with a particular topical category in applied ethics, see the suggestions below.

Abortion

Execution of an Abortion-Provider's Killer   31
Fetal Rights and the Fetus as Person: The Case of J.D.S.   40
Fetal Rights, Take Two: Unborn Victims of Violence Act   41
Zero Population Growth   44
Fetal Testing for Down Syndrome   57
License-Plate Liberties   120

Animals

'A Hunting We Will Go . . .   74
GloFish   75
Dolphin Parks   81
Eating Sea Turtles   85
Canned Hunts   92
Cosmetic Surgery for Pets   94
O Canada, How Could You?   97

Capital Punishment

Stanley "Tookie" Williams and the Problem of Redemption   14
The Execution of Scott Hain, Juvenile Offender   15
Bible Used in Conviction   18

Execution of an Abortion-Provider's Killer   31

Medical Care for Prisoners, Take Three: Organ Transplant for Death
Row Inmate   54

Civil Disobedience

Three Nuns and a Silo   26

Edward "NJ Weedman" Forchion: Ganja Brings Him Closer to God   117

Environment

Zero Population Growth   44

Age-Based Cost Studies   51

Age-Extension Research   60

Famine in Ethiopia   70

'A Hunting We Will Go . . .   74

Ecoterrorism: Kill the Hummers!   77

Dolphin Parks   81

Eating Sea Turtles   85

PBDE and the Precautionary Principle   88

My Hummer, My Choice   132

Ethics and Business

White-Collar Crime   32

White-Collar Crime, Take Two: Atlantic States Foundry   34

Troublesome Trinkets   68

Canned Hunts   92

Obesity: Personal or Political?   108

Wal-Mart Keeps Its Shelves Clean   114

Extreme Makeover   158

Ethics and Medicine

Chemical Castration for Male Sex Offenders   20

Fetal Rights and the Fetus as Person: The Case of J.D.S.   40

Fetal Rights, Take Two: Unborn Victims of Violence Act   41
Zero Population Growth   44
Growth Hormones for Shortness   48
Medical Care for Prisoners   53
Medical Care for Prisoners, Take Two: Donor Heart
    Goes to a Criminal   53
Medical Care for Prisoners, Take Three: Organ Transplant for Death
    Row Inmate   54
Fetal Testing for Down Syndrome   57
Age-Extension Research   60
The Schiavos   64
Obesity: Personal or Political?   108
Ed Rosenthal and Medical Marijuana   123
Extreme Makeover   158

Future Generations

Zero Population Growth   44
Age-Extension Research   60
My Hummer, My Choice   132

Global Justice

Zero Population Growth   44
Troublesome Trinkets   68
Famine in Ethiopia   70
My Hummer, My Choice   132

Individual Liberty

Zero Population Growth   44
DanceSafe: Making Ecstasy Safer for Partyers   102
Banning Ephedra   104
Obesity: Personal or Political?   108
Worried about Harry Potter   112

Wal-Mart Keeps Its Shelves Clean   114
Edward "NJ Weedman" Forchion: Ganja Brings Him
    Closer to God   117
License-Plate Liberties   120
Pledge of Allegiance   120
Ed Rosenthal and Medical Marijuana   123
High School Tells Student to Remove Anti-War Shirt   127
My Hummer, My Choice   132
"Let Those Who Ride Decide": Motorcycle Helmet Laws
    and Biker Rights   133
USA Patriot Act   135
Evolution vs. Creationism in Public Schools   147
Creationism, Take Two: Professor Dini's Recommendation   151

Lying, Cheating, and Stealing

Stealing from the Wishing Well   28
White-Collar Crime   32
White-Collar Crime, Take Two: Atlantic States Foundry   34
Sports Supplementation: Fair or Foul?   153
Extreme Makeover   158
Rigoberta Menchú: The Purpose of Truth   174

Physician-Assisted Suicide/Euthanasia

Elder Suicide or Dignified Exit? A Letter from Ohio   38
Suicide Concert   47
The Schiavos   64

Privacy

Vicarious Sensitization   22
Fetal Rights, Take Three: Drug Abuse and Fetal Abuse   42
Zero Population Growth   44
Banning Ephedra   104

Edward "NJ Weedman" Forchion: Ganja Brings Him
     Closer to God   117
Cameras Watching Students   125
CRACK—Get Sterilized, Get Cash   129
USA Patriot Act   135

Religion and Morality

Bible Used in Conviction   18
Worried about Harry Potter   112
Edward "NJ Weedman" Forchion: Ganja Brings Him
     Closer to God   117
Pledge of Allegiance   120
Same-Sex Unions and the Defense of Marriage   140
Sex Education in School   145
Evolution vs. Creationism in Public Schools   147
Culture Wars   160
Bright Rights   163
Character Education of Children   168
Character Education, Take Two: Georgia's "Respect for the
     Creator" Principle   173

Risk Assessment

Zero Population Growth   44
Fetal Testing for Down Syndrome   57
PBDE and the Precautionary Principle   88
Banning Ephedra   104

Science and Technology

Age-Extension Research   60
GloFish   75
PBDE and the Precautionary Principle   88

Sex and Love and Marriage

CRACK—Get Sterilized, Get Cash   129
Same-Sex Unions and the Defense of Marriage   140
Gay Sex and Adultery   144
Sex Education in School   145
Extreme Makeover   158

War and Terrorism

Ecoterrorism: Kill the Hummers!   77
War Is Terrorism   81
High School Tells Student to Remove Anti-War Shirt   127
USA Patriot Act   135

Theory-Based
Table of Contents

If you are interested in cases that suggest the application of a particular theoretical approach or that highlight the tension between types of theoretical approach, see the suggestions below.

Utilitarianism/Consequentialism

Torture of a Kidnapper   24
White-Collar Crime   32
White-Collar Crime, Take Two: Atlantic States Foundry   34
Zero Population Growth   44
Age-Based Cost Studies   51
Age-Extension Research   60
Troublesome Trinkets   68
PBDE and the Precautionary Principle   88
DanceSafe: Making Ecstasy Safer for Partyers   102
Cameras Watching Students   125
USA Patriot Act   135
Rigoberta Menchú: The Purpose of Truth   174

Deontology/Kantianism/Categorical Imperative

Stanley "Tookie" Williams and the Problem of Redemption   14
The Execution of Scott Hain, Juvenile Offender   15
Torture of a Kidnapper   24
Fetal Rights and the Fetus as Person: The Case of J.D.S.   40

Suicide Concert   47
Fetal Testing for Down Syndrome   57
The Schiavos   64
Famine in Ethiopia   70
GloFish   75
Ecoterrorism: Kill the Hummers!   77
Same-Sex Unions and the Defense of Marriage   140
Sex Education in School   145
Rigoberta Menchú: The Purpose of Truth   174

Virtue Theory

Stanley "Tookie" Williams and the Problem of Redemption   14
Canned Hunts   92
My Hummer, My Choice   132
Gay Sex and Adultery   144
Sex Education in School   145
Sports Supplementation: Fair or Foul?   153
Sports Supplementation, Take Two: Ross Rebagliati   157
Extreme Makeover   158
Culture Wars   160
Ethics for the Information Age: The SCANS Report   166
Character Education of Children   168

Biocentrism/Ecocentrism

Zero Population Growth   44
GloFish   75
Ecoterrorism: Kill the Hummers!   77
Dolphin Parks   81
Eating Sea Turtles   85
PBDE and the Precautionary Principle   88
Canned Hunts   92

O Canada, How Could You?   97
My Hummer, My Choice   132

Evolution/Sociobiology

Age-Extension Research   60
Evolution vs. Creationism in Public Schools   147
Creationism, Take Two: Professor Dini's Recommendation   151

Justice

Retributive Justice

Stanley "Tookie" Williams and the Problem of Redemption   14
The Execution of Scott Hain, Juvenile Offender   15
Chemical Castration for Male Sex Offenders   20
Vicarious Sensitization   22
The Consenting Victim   29
White-Collar Crime   32
White-Collar Crime, Take Two: Atlantic States Foundry   34
Fetal Rights, Take Two: Unborn Victims of Violence Act   41

Distributive Justice

Zero Population Growth   44
Medical Care for Prisoners   53
Medical Care for Prisoners, Take Two: Donor Heart
    Goes to a Criminal   53
Medical Care for Prisoners, Take Three: Organ Transplant
    for Death Row Inmate   54
Troublesome Trinkets   68
My Hummer, My Choice   132

Relativism

Bible Used in Conviction   18
Eating Sea Turtles   85

Sex Education in School   145
Culture Wars   160
A Call to Civil Society   165
Ethics for the Information Age: The SCANS Report   166

Ethical Egoism

My Hummer, My Choice   132

Principle-Based Table of Contents

If you are interested in exploring a particular moral principle (such as justice or compassion or nonmaleficence), check some of the suggestions below.

Justice

Stanley "Tookie" Williams and the Problem of Redemption   14

The Execution of Scott Hain, Juvenile Offender   15

White-Collar Crime   32

Medical Care for Prisoners   53

Medical Care for Prisoners, Take Two: Donor Heart
Goes to a Criminal   53

Medical Care for Prisoners, Take Three: Organ Transplant
for Death Row Inmate   54

Troublesome Trinkets   68

Sports Supplementation: Fair or Foul?   153

Respect for Autonomy

Chemical Castration for Male Sex Offenders   20

The Consenting Victim   29

Elder Suicide or Dignified Exit? A Letter from Ohio   38

Fetal Rights and the Fetus as Person: The Case of J.D.S.   40

Zero Population Growth   44

Suicide Concert   47

Banning Ephedra   104
CRACK—Get Sterilized, Get Cash   129

Beneficence

Elder Suicide or Dignified Exit? A Letter from Ohio   38
Growth Hormones for Shortness   48
Fetal Testing for Down Syndrome   57
Age Extension Research   60
The Schiavos   64
DanceSafe: Making Ecstasy Safer for Partiers   102

Nonmaleficence (do no harm)

Chemical Castration for Male Sex Offenders   20
Vicarious Sensitization   22
Zero Population Growth   44
Growth Hormones for Shortness   48
The Schiavos   64
Troublesome Trinkets   68
GloFish   75
Dolphin Parks   81
PBDE and the Precautionary Principle   88
Canned Hunts   92

Acknowledgments

I would like to thank the following colleagues for their insightful comments, which helped shape the direction of this project from its early inception:

Rawda Awwad, *Pittsburgh Technical Institute*

Brian Bix, *University of Minnesota*

Candace Gauthier, *University of North Carolina—Wilmington*

Robert Hambourger, *North Carolina State University*

Paul Leclerc, *Community College of Rhode Island*

Donna J. Werner, *St. Louis Community College—Meramec*

David Yount, *Mesa Community College*

I'd also like to thank the following reviewers for their valuable feedback:

Mohammad Azadpur, *San Francisco State University*

Daniel Barwick, *Alfred State College*

Gayle Brown, *Santa Fe Community College*

Michael Buratovich, *Spring Arbor University*

Matthew Calarco, *Sweet Briar College*

Christopher Ciocchetti, *Centenary College of Louisiana*

Susan Claxton, *Floyd College*

Jonathan Cohen, *University of Maine—Farmington*

Richard Combes, *University of South Carolina—Spartanburg*

Graham Dixon, *DeVry University*

Laura Ekstrom, *College of William and Mary*

Steven Emmanuel, *Virginia Wesleyan College*

Stephen Finlay, *University of Southern California*
Gregory Fried, *California State University—Los Angeles*
Thomas Gilbert, *Morningside College*
Carla Grady, *Santa Rosa Junior College*
Laura Grams, *University of Nebraska—Omaha*
Christopher Grau, *Florida International University*
Gael Grossman, *Jamestown Community College*
James Hanink, *Loyola Marymount University*
Craig Hanks, *Texas State University*
George Harris, *College of William and Mary*
Christian Hipp, *Midlands Technical College*
Seth Holtzman, *Catawba College*
Jerri Killian, *Wright State University*
A. David Kline, *University of North Florida*
J. Steven Kramer, *Southwest Minnesota State University*
Jordan Lindberg, *Central Michigan University*
Richard Lippke, *James Madison University*
Phillip Long, *Grace Bible College*
Robert Lovering, *American University*
Dale Lugenbehl, *Lane Community College*
Tim Madigan, *Rochester Institute of Technology*
Miriam McCormick, *University of Richmond*
Peter Mehl, *University of Central Arkansas*
David Merli, *Franklin and Marshall College*
Leroy Meyer, *University of South Dakota*
Chris Meyers, *Southern Methodist University*
Toska Olson, *Evergreen State College*
David O'Shaughnessy, *Los Angeles Harbor College*
Matthew Pamental, *University of Utah*
Andrew Pavelich, *University of Houston—Downtown*
Thomas Peard, *Baker University*
Gaile Pohlhaus, *Miami University*

Christopher Preston, *University of South Carolina*
Shari Prior, *College of Saint Mary*
Larry Reinhart, *Malone College*
Terrence Reynolds, *Georgetown University*
Norbert Schedler, *University of Central Arkansas*
David Schwartz, *Randolph-Macon Woman's College*
Marla Selvidge, *Central Missouri State University*
William Lad Sessions, *Washington and Lee University*
Andrew Simon, *Portland Community College*
John Sniegocki, *Xavier University*
Barbara Solheim, *Harper College*
Phillip Spivey, *University of Central Arkansas*
Anita Superson, *University of Kentucky*
Eve Szalay, *Weber State University*
Stephen Taylor, *Delaware State University*
Brad Thompson, *Southern Methodist University*
Jon Tresan, *University of Florida*
Mark van Roojen, *University of Nebraska—Lincoln*

Thank you to dialogue partners Roger and Alexandra Pierce, whose dining room provided the inspiration for a parlor game called *Morality Play* and who offered a multitude of suggestions on the text. I would also like to express my heartfelt gratitude to Jon-David Hague and Allison Rona at McGraw-Hill, for their gracious support.

Introduction

Why Think about Morality?
Using Case Studies to Think about Morality
Morality Play
Ethical Argumentation (and Arguing Ethically)
Pluralism, Relativism, and Absolutism
A Quick Review of Critical Thinking

◤◤ WHY THINK ABOUT MORALITY?

You have undoubtedly been a moral philosopher at one time or another. Perhaps you worried about whether to break a promise or give away a secret when there seemed to be a compelling reason for doing so. In an election you supported a clean environment as more important than a strong economy, though your father was out of work. Perhaps you have debated with family and friends on issues such as abortion, capital punishment, sex education in schools, and global warming.

But isn't philosophy more abstract than this? Isn't it the pursuit of wisdom for its own sake? The search for an understanding of the nature of reality? The search for the grounds of morality—for the meaning of right and wrong, good and evil, rather than for everyday answers? Yes, philosophy is about all that. But *moral* philosophy is also practical, aimed at determining how best to live from day to day in an ever-changing world. Moral philosophy is about making deliberate, conscious choices in both the mundane challenges of daily life and the more extraordinary quandaries that humans often face. It is also about developing certain personal qualities and not others, working in one career rather than another, relating in certain ways and not others to our friends, family, neighbors, and fellow citizens.

Moral choices are choices that matter, that will affect others in some way, small or large. When it comes down to it, almost all our choices do affect others. It may be that the choice of which shirt to wear today matters little, but the choice of which shirt to buy probably matters to some degree. Do I shop at The Gap because I like the styles? Or do I avoid buying goods from all corporations whose manufacturing practices are morally questionable? (And, if so, am I willing to go naked?) Sometimes we respond passively to moral situations by letting momentum or other people push us along or by being unaware that something as simple as our shopping list may affect other people. But even such passivity must be recognized as choice. Although we might not want to go as far as Socrates and say that the unexamined life is not worth living, it's true that a rich, full, thoughtful life requires attention to the moral aspect of human existence.

Morality involves establishing a considered point of view about what is right and wrong, good and bad. As we mature into adults, we go through a complex mental and emotional process—often a grueling one—to develop such sensibilities. Trying to be a moral person requires work because the moral dimension of life is complex and nuanced. And although some moral challenges are easily resolved, many are not. So, how do we prepare ourselves?

One way is to apply conscious effort to developing our moral sensibilities by thinking critically about a whole range of moral problems that divide well-meaning people. Moral judgment is shaped by disciplined thought and fostered by repeated practice. We might liken morality to physical fitness. To maintain a level of health, we must exercise regularly; to improve involves even more sweat and tears and some time on the track or in the gym. Similarly, we can do strengthening exercises to keep moral muscles limber and strong. One such exercise is the case study.

USING CASE STUDIES TO THINK ABOUT MORALITY

In this book you will find a series of vignettes, events, proposals, technologies, and news stories, each of which presents a conflict of values. These items vary widely in topic, but all concern how we ought best to live together. Some call on our individual conscience (for example, questions of responsible consumption), others on our social conscience (should capital punishment be legal? abortion?). All of them address issues of importance; all are drawn from real events. They are called "case studies."

A case study plucks a moral problem out of the teeming chaos of life and isolates it in a fishbowl—behind glass, apart from relatives and friends—so that we can examine it up close. The case study presents a discrete problem through which we can engage our abstract notions about morality. General ethical rules, which may enjoy near universal support are actually subject to a great deal of interpretation. We all may agree that it is wrong to kill innocent people. But are enemy soldiers innocent? Are day-old fetuses people?

Case studies are indispensable in the study of law, business, and medicine. In moral inquiry, they have a longer but more checkered history. Although it had been a venerable art for many centuries, casuistry (the analysis of specific cases) degenerated during the 16th and 17th centuries into a method of elaborately building excuses and justifications for doing bad things. Casuistry's tarnished reputation caused it to be largely ignored during the development of modern philosophy—until recently, when the art and science of the case study began to enjoy a renaissance.

Moral philosophy has focused much of its attention on the articulation of principles such as justice, respect for autonomy, avoiding harm, and benefiting others. These core principles enjoy broad support. But the interpreting and applying them support. It is one thing to give an abstract definition of justice that would find broad support in everyday life: let's say "giving each person his or her due." But what is due to whom, and why? Is capital punishment what is due to someone like Scott Hain, who committed a brutal crime at the age of 17? (see the second case in the Crime and Punishment section). Cases serve to practice reasoning and to work toward the specification of abstract principles in relation to the concrete cases.

The cases in this book are not fictional: They are drawn from newspaper accounts, legal opinions, and other factual sources, and most of them involve real, very cold, and uncomfortable consequences. They are meant to test such generalizations as "do not lie" and "do not kill" by generating thought and dialogue about concrete events that can alter the way a person chooses to live, day by day. If the issue of exploitation of sweatshop workers is troubling to us, we may become conscious of where and how we shop.

MORALITY PLAY

There are many ways to use these cases, but they have been particularly designed as the basis for a game called *Morality Play*. The two most obvious places to play this game are in the classroom and at get-togethers of friends and family.

Participants will take turns being the moderator. Agree on some fair method for choosing the sequence of moderators. Players may forfeit their turn as moderator if they wish. The moderator begins by reading the chosen (or assigned) case out loud. He or she may want to read it more than once so that players can absorb the relevant details.

The moderator is then responsible for engaging the group in discussion—asking probing questions, seeking clarification of statements, asking particular players to explain their positions in more detail: doing whatever is necessary to encourage a civil, provocative discussion. Each case includes a list of discussion questions that can be used to guide discussion, if desired. Or the moderator can devise his or her own questions. A turn is up when the moderator, with the agreement of the group, feels that the case has been thoroughly mined. Depending on the group, the time spent may be as short as five minutes or as long as an hour or more. Then switch moderators and move on to a new case.

Morality Play works best with a group of four to six, so a large class should be broken down into manageable units. Two can play; interestingly enough, this tends to produce intense dialogue. A solo game adds the challenge of forcing the player to imagine all sides of an issue for him- or herself. A solo game will be particularly enjoyable if the player writes down thoughts and then deliberately takes other viewpoints. When we have to articulate our thoughts, either aloud or on paper, we move closer to clarity.

The Resources section at the end of each case study provides a list of readings.

The Rules of *Morality Play*

1. Elaborate your arguments and conclusion, don't just state them.

2. Listen carefully to your fellow players. Try to understand their point of view.

3. Players may ask other players to clarity a statement or position.

4. Aim for dialogue—a back-and-forth among players. The moderator can encourage those who are hesitant to speak and hold back those who monopolize the conversation.

5. The following statements (and others of the same variety) are off-limits during play because they are conversation stoppers: "That's just my opinion." "Just because!"

6. Stick to ideas. Watch out for personal attacks: "Only a moron would hold such a belief" or "You are obviously a misogynistic pig." There are graceful ways to undermine silly or offensive beliefs.

7. Play fair. Avoid tricking other players by using any logical fallacies (see below if you need to remind yourself). Persuade others of your point of view by making its reasonableness shine forth.

8. Be humble. Don't engage in clever rhetoric just so you sound smart.

ETHICAL ARGUMENTATION (AND ARGUING ETHICALLY)

Argumentation in ethics aims to explore and justify a possible decision, course of action, or point of view. We seek to justify that a belief or position is reasonable. To this end, we engage shared principles, factual information, and logical, coherent, *reasonable* argument. A conflict of opinion is usually not a conflict over basic values (that torture is wrong, say) but over the application of the general rules in a particular case. Is torture wrong even when, as in the case of Jakob von Metzler (the sixth case in Crime and Punishment), it might lead a kidnapper to reveal the whereabouts of an innocent boy whose life is in danger? Ethical argumentation doesn't necessarily resolve an issue—we may still disagree about torturing the kidnapper—but through discussion each participant reexamines, refines, and adjusts his or her attitudes and assumptions.

Particular cases often form the basis for a broader social debate. For example, the case of J.D.S., an institutionalized mentally handicapped woman who was raped and became pregnant, has become the focal point of a social and legal debate over abortion and the status of the fetus. Is J.D.S.'s guardian also the guardian of the fetus? Or is the fetus a person with interests of its own, deserving of a separate guardian for those interests? Who should decide whether an abortion is to be performed?

Discussing moral problems involves an inner process of self-examination and mental clarification, and we may change our present beliefs. We may begin by trying to persuade others of our Truth, but as we expand, refine, and alter our own conceptions, we develop a more critical, more thoughtful view of things than the one we had when we started.

There is, of course, a strong element of persuasion involved: when we feel strongly about a certain moral point of view, we want to bring others around to see things as we do. But this is not our sole agenda. Ethical argumentation itself needs to be ethical. That is, we agree to be fair, play by the rules, and work toward mutual understanding.

PLURALISM, RELATIVISM, AND ABSOLUTISM

Ethics doesn't allow for the exactness of geometry, where there is (usually) one correct solution to a given problem. This leads some people to feel that dialogue about moral problems is an exercise in futility. "Let's just all agree to disagree," they'll say, "and leave it at that." But the fact that ethics is fuzzy does not mean that there is no method to the madness of argument. Practical reasoning—what Aristotle called *phronesis*—is action oriented. We reason so that we may act well. The conclusions we reach are not true in an enduring way (as 2 plus 2 always equals 4), but they can be sensible and plausible at a particular point in time. And they can be understood as sensible and plausible by other people.

Moral values are fluid—but not so fluid that they simply wash down the drain, which is what happens when one subscribes to a crude (but common) form of relativism, where values are nothing more than one person's opinion. And it is precisely the thickness of moral values that makes discourse important. After all, there is no reason to talk about moral issues if one view is as good as another—better just get out your stick and convince people by hitting them with it. However, dogmatic absolutism can be dangerous as well as self-righteous.

Religious justifications are sometimes lumped into the category of "absolutisms" and are shrugged off by "rational" philosophers. However, many people hold that moral values spring from religious beliefs about the world and that we should not deny these foundations. Indeed, these foundational beliefs should be respected as part of reasonable dialogue. Those who hold strong religious beliefs are often the first to note that interpretation and independent personal reflection are necessary. After all, religious texts are notoriously ambiguous. And even where they are clear, they require interpretation. The Bible commands us not to kill and also commands us to punish with death those who murder another man. To which command should we adhere, under what circumstances, and why? Religious belief can get people into trouble when it becomes rigid—and be an excuse to avoid dialogue and self-examination.

A common claim is "Oh, well, you don't have any experience with this issue, so your opinion is invalid." This sometimes happens, for example, with the abortion discussion, when the opinions of men are dismissed as intrusive and illegitimate. But direct experience is not a prerequisite for sound moral judgment. Most of us, as we consider capital punishment, for example, have never committed a serious crime. And consider this: men do face issues related to abortion. Not all of them take responsibility for their part in an unexpected or unwanted pregnancy; but many do. And men are both lawmakers and citizens, creating and obeying the nation's laws. Having an abortion and enacting capital punishment are moral choices with which an entire society is involved.

A QUICK REVIEW OF CRITICAL THINKING

An **argument** is not a quarrel but a piece of reasoning aimed at making point or offering a conclusion. Typically, an argument will have at least one premise and a conclusion. The premises offer reasons for the conclusion. A good argument is one in which the conclusion follows from the premises and in which the premises are true or at least warranted.

A **fallacy** is an error in reasoning. Such error can be quite persuasive, when the fallacy goes unnoticed. The following fallacies are commonly found hiding in discussions:

> *Argumentum ad hominem*—Argument "against the person" rather than the person's ideas. ("Of course he's wrong. He wears his pants too tight.")

Argumentum ad ignorantiam—Argument "from ignorance." Claiming that a proposition is true if it hasn't been proven false. ("There is no life on Mars. No one has ever been able to find any.")

Argumentum ad populam—"Appeal to the people." Something is true because "everybody thinks so." ("Everyone knows that diet pills are the fastest way to lose weight.")

Argumentum ad verecundiam—"Appeal to authority." The testimony of someone believed to be an authority is called upon in support of a conclusion. It is important to distinguish between an appeal to unqualified authority (a fallacy) and a reasonable appeal to qualified authority in support of evidence. ("Ephedra is completely safe—it says so on the Ephedra Education Council's Web site.")

Equivocation—Deliberate confusion of two or more meanings of the same word, where the word is used to mean one thing in a premise and another thing in the conclusion. ("All banks are besides rivers. Therefore, the bank where I deposit my money has a great water supply.")

False dichotomy—Mistaken assumption that there are only two possible solutions to a problem or that we must choose between only two alternatives. ("People or nature!" "Jobs or spotted owls!")

Faulty analogy—An argument that because two things are alike in some respects, they will also be alike in other respects. ("When a woman is raped and becomes pregnant, the fetus is like a stranger intruding on her body. Just as it is justifiable to kill a stranger in self-defense, it is justifiable to have an abortion after a rape results in pregnancy.")

Hasty generalization—A generalization is formed on the basis of limited data. ("Eight high school shootings were committed by boys who watched violent video games. These games obviously incite violent behavior and should be outlawed.")

Petitio principii—"Begging the question," or assuming the conclusion as part of a premise. The premise and conclusion say the same thing in different words. ("Capital punishment is wrong because it is murder.")

Post hoc ergo propter hoc—"After this, therefore because of this." The claim that one thing is caused by another simply because it follows from the other. ("There are more people in prison than ever before in U.S. history. Therefore, we have the best police force we've ever had.")

Red herring fallacy—Diverting attention by going off on extraneous points. ("Sex education in schools will lead to increased teen sexual activity. Already, the availability of condoms in Maryland high schools over the past three years has led to higher rates of sex among students.")

Slippery slope—A claim that a chain of causal events will occur; if we allow one kind of practice, other horrible practices will follow (where it is unproven whether the chain of events will occur). ("If any more nations back out of the Kyoto Treaty on global warming, we'll never be able to have an effective international treaty to protect the environment.")

Straw man—Attacking a distortion of an opponent's position, rather than his or her position. ("She supports the preservation of the snail darter even though it will cost some jobs. She must hate people.")

Resources and Bibliography for the Introduction

ARISTOTLE. 1962. *Nicomachean Ethics*. Translated, with an introduction and notes, by Martin Oswald. Indianapolis: Bobbs-Merrill.

AUDI, ROBERT. 1989. *Practical Reasoning*. New York: Routledge.

BECK, ROBERT N., and JOHN B. ORR. 1970. *Ethical Choice: A Case Study Approach*. New York: The Free Press.

BEDAU, HUGO ADAM. 1997. *Mortal Choices: Three Exercises in Moral Casuistry*. New York: Oxford University Press.

BURCH, ROBERT W. 1997. *A Concise Introduction to Logic*. 6th ed. Belmont, CA: Wadsworth.

JONSEN, ALBERT, and STEPHEN TOULMIN. 1988. *The Abuse of Casuistry: A History of Moral Reasoning*. Berkeley: University of California Press.

KAHANE, HOWARD, and NANCY CAVENDER. 2002. *Logic and Contemporary Rhetoric*. 9th ed. Belmont, CA: Wadsworth.

LANHAM, RICHARD A. 1991. *Handbook of Rhetorical Terms*. 2nd ed. Berkeley: University of California Press.

MILLER, RICHARD B. 1996. *Casuistry in Modern Ethics*. Chicago: The University of Chicago Press.

PARKER, MICHAEL, and DONNA DICKENSON. 2001. *The Cambridge Medical Ethics Workbook*. Cambridge: Cambridge University Press.

PAUL, RICHARD W. 1993. *Critical Thinking: What Every Person Needs to Survive in a Rapidly Changing World*. 3rd ed. Santa Rosa, CA: Foundation for Critical Thinking.

PENCE, GREGORY E. 2000. *Classic Cases in Medical Ethics*. 3rd ed. New York: McGraw-Hill.

STEVENS, EDWARD. 1997. *Developing Moral Imagination: Case Studies in Practical Morality*. Kansas City: Sheed & Ward.

WALTON, DOUGLAS. 2003. *Ethical Argumentation*. Lanham, MD: Lexington Books.

Crime and *Punishment*

I

Stanley "Tookie" Williams and the Problem of Redemption

The Execution of Scott Hain, Juvenile Offender

Bible Used in Conviction

Chemical Castration for Male Sex Offenders

Vicarious Sensitization

Torture of a Kidnapper

Three Nuns and a Silo

Stealing from the Wishing Well

The Consenting Victim

Execution of an Abortion-Provider's Killer

White-Collar Crime

White-Collar Crime, Take Two: Atlantic States Foundry

◤◤ STANLEY "TOOKIE" WILLIAMS AND THE PROBLEM OF REDEMPTION

From his cell in San Quentin prison, Stanley "Tookie" Williams does what he can to make the world a better place. Williams, who has been on death row for more than 20 years, spends his time trying to lure kids away from a life of gangs. He is familiar with them: In 1981, Williams, along with a friend, started the infamous Crips gang in South Central Los Angeles. When he was 26, Williams was convicted of murdering four people during two attempted robberies (a crime for which he has never admitted guilt). He was sentenced to death. During his 20-odd years in prison, Williams has witnessed an enormous growth in gang membership and violence. The Crips gang has grown in power, and many copycat gangs have sprouted up in other cities.

Stanley Williams is trying to make amends. Among other things, he has written eight books for teenagers and started the Internet Project for Street Peace, which reaches out to children not only in the inner cities of the United States but all over the world. Williams provides what many inner-city teens lack: a positive role model. He tries to convince them that they need to believe in themselves—that they are good people and can accomplish good things in the world. In his "Letter to Incarcerated Youth, No. 1," Tookie writes,

> It's time to flip the script. You and I can complain 24X7 about the problems of poverty, drugs, violence, racism and other injustices, but unless we choose to initiate a personal change, we will remain puppets of unjust conditions. Unless *we* change, we will be incapable of changing the circumstances around us.
>
> —(www.tookie.com)

And by all accounts, Williams has had an enormous influence. Indeed, his work has been notable enough to earn him a nomination for a Nobel Peace Prize.

Many believe that the governor of California should commute Williams's sentence to life in prison to reward his good works. Others think that redemption is not the issue—that punishment should be meted out according to the crime, not according to whether a criminal develops a conscience after the fact. They think that Williams is still a murderer and must still pay for his crime, as an example to others.

Discussion Questions

1. Should remorse, rehabilitation, and redemption play any role in what punishment a person receives? Or is the punishment simply a response to the crime, and nothing more?

2. Has Williams redeemed himself through good works?

3. Should Williams still be put to death?

4. Is it appropriate for someone who has done very bad things to be rewarded with one of the world's highest honors?

Resources

Stanley "Tookie" Williams's Web site. www.tookie.com.
WILLIAMS, STANLEY, with BARBARA COTTMAN BECNAL. 2001. *Life in Prison*. New York: SeaStar Books.
WILLIAMS, STANLEY, with BARBARA COTTMAN BECNAL. 2001, 2003. *Tookie Speaks Out Against Gang Violence* (eight readers aimed at urban youth). New York: Powerkids Press.

THE EXECUTION OF SCOTT HAIN, JUVENILE OFFENDER

On October 6, 1987, 17-year-old Scott Hain and his friend Robert Lambert were out drinking and looking for trouble in Tulsa, Oklahoma. They spotted a young couple sitting in their car in a parking lot outside a restaurant. Hain and Lambert hijacked the car, with the couple in it. After some time, Hain and Lambert stopped the car, robbed the man and woman, and then shoved them into the car's trunk. Lambert then set fire to the car, burning the man and woman alive.

Scott Hain, a juvenile at the time of his offense, was convicted of felony murder. In April 2003, 16 years later, Hain was finally executed by lethal injection in the state of Oklahoma. Lambert is currently still on death row.

Currently, 28 of the 50 states in the United States have statutes prohibiting the execution of juveniles, that is, anyone under the age of 18. In many states where juveniles can legally be executed, no executions have in fact been carried out. Since 1976, there have been 21 executions of juveniles, 13 of these in Texas alone. The constitutionality of executing juvenile offenders was reviewed by the U.S. Supreme Court in 1988 (in *Thompson v. Oklahoma*) and again in 1989 (in *Stanford v. Kentucky*). In 1988 the Court held that "evolving standards of decency that mark the progress of a maturing society" dictated that offenders 15 years old and younger should not be executed. And in 1989, the Court held that the Eighth Amendment, which prohibits "usual and unusual punishment," does not prohibit the execution of 16- and 17-year old offenders. In 2002, the Supreme Court appeared ready to revisit the issue of juvenile execution. In the case *In re Kevin Nigel Stanford*, four of the justices signed a joint statement calling capital punishment for juveniles a "shameful practice." Yet a year later the Court declined to review Hain's case (*Hain v. Mullen*, 2003).

Opponents of the death penalty for juvenile offenders argue that "evolving standards of decency" do, indeed, indicate a strong social aversion to executing juveniles, pointing to the fact that even among those states that allow juvenile execution, it is rarely carried through. They note that international consensus strongly opposes the practice. The International Justice Project cites the United Nations Convention on the Rights of the Child, which prohibits the execution of juvenile offenders. (The United States has not signed this treaty.) Only five countries are known to have executed juveniles since 1990: Iran, Saudi Arabia, Yemen, Pakistan, and the United States.

Those who support the execution of juvenile offenders argue that social consensus has not, in fact, changed dramatically. The moral soundness of any punishment, including capital punishment, is generally based on the idea that punishment should be proportionate both to the seriousness of the crime and to the culpability of the offender. Those who support the execution of 16- and 17-year-old capital offenders—typically murderers—argue that at 16 or 17 a person can act autonomously enough to be held responsible for his or her actions and that the maturity of an offender would need to be judged case by case. Although age may be a mitigating factor in assigning punishment, it is not (unlike mental retardation) an absolute standard for making judgments. Opponents argue that because of their emotional and cognitive immaturity, juveniles are not as culpable as adults. Recent research indicates that the human brain undergoes rapid development during the adolescent years, particularly in the parts of the brain that control impulses and emotions, leaving teenagers less capable of consciously controlling their behavior than adults. Psychiatric research suggests that childhood trauma from neglect and abuse causes physical changes in the brain, often leading to violent behavior. Some people have argued, on these grounds, that Scott Hain's chaotic childhood and family background should be considered mitigating factors. His parents were both heavy drinkers who offered their children little positive guidance or nurturing. Hain's father introduced him to marijuana at age 9 or 10.

Discussion Questions

1. Should Scott Hain have been executed?

2. Should the United States look to national standards regarding capital punishment for juvenile offenders, or does international consensus constitute an "evolving standard" to which we should adhere?

3. Is capital punishment a just and appropriate punishment for adult offenders?

4. Was the delay of 16 years between Hain's conviction and his execution cruel?

Resources

CASSEL, ELAINE. 2003. "Did the Malvo Case Influence the Supreme Court on Juvenile Executions?" *CNN.com,* February 11.

GREENHOUSE, LINDA. 2003. "Justices Deny Inmate Appeal in Execution of Juveniles."*New York Times,* January 28, A19.

The International Justice Project, information on juvenile execution. See, particularly, "Brain Development, Culpability and the Death Penalty." www.internationaljusticeproject.org/juveniles.cfm.

BIBLE USED IN CONVICTION

By all accounts, Robert Harlan's crime was a heinous one. He was convicted in 1995 in Colorado of kidnapping, raping, and murdering a young woman and shooting—and leaving paralyzed—another woman who had stopped to help the first. Judge John J. Vigil, who sentenced Harlan, noted that his crimes were among the most horrible he had ever seen and admitted that the death penalty was utterly justified. Yet Vigil felt compelled to overturn Harlan's death sentence. The reason: some of the sequestered jurors had used their hotel Bibles during deliberation over sentencing. Although it is unclear whether Bibles were actually carried into the deliberation room, several jurors had handwritten notes with scriptural passages that support the death penalty (in particular, Leviticus 24:20–21, "fracture for fracture, eye for eye, tooth for tooth; as he has disfigured a man, he shall be disfigured. He who kills a beast shall make it good; and he who kills a man shall be put to death."). Since biblical code is not part of Colorado law, the use of these passages, according to Harlan's defense team, was improper. According to the judge, it was unconstitutional because the verdict had been unduly influenced. Prosecutors countered that sequestering jurors means shielding them from media, not filtering out their own moral beliefs.

Discussion Questions

1. Was the judge right to consider the use of a Bible in a jury deliberation an "undue" influence?

2. If a juror knew a biblical passage by heart (e.g., the Leviticus 24 passage) and cited it as his or her moral belief during deliberation, would this be different from carrying into the deliberation room a scrap of paper with the Leviticus passage scribbled on it? What if the passage in question was from a "nonreligious" source like Stephen King's *The Green Mile*?

3. Should deeply religious people be banned from jury duty?

4. Can religious belief serve as a foundation for morality in a pluralistic society?

5. Do jurors have a more fundamental commitment to biblical law or to Colorado law?

6. Juries are asked, "Can you decide this case in conformity to U.S. law?" But is there not a higher law of right and wrong?

Resources

WorldNetDaily. 2003. "Judge Kills Death Sentence Because Jurors Read Bible." May 24. www.worldnetdaily.com/news/article.asp? ARTICLE_ ID=32747 (accessed January 14, 2004).

CHEMICAL CASTRATION FOR MALE SEX OFFENDERS

Sexual assault is considered the most rapidly growing violent crime in America: In 2002, some 248,000 sexual assaults were reported to the police. According to the Rape, Abuse, and Incest National Network, someone in the United States is sexually assaulted every two minutes. One in every six women will be raped during her lifetime. The number of children who are sexually molested each year is uncertain, but the Justice Department estimates that one of every six victims of sexual assault is younger than 12.

Section 645 of the California Penal Code reads:

> Any person guilty of a first conviction of [specified sexual offenses], where the victim has not attained 13 years of age, may, upon parole, undergo medroxyprogesterone acetate treatment or its chemical equivalent, in addition to other punishment prescribed for that offense or any other provision of law, at the discretion of the court.

In 1996, California became the first state to approve the use of "chemical castration." California law mandates that sex offenders convicted more than once of child molestation will be injected with Depo-Provera or some other testosterone-reducing drug, with the intention of reducing their sex drive. The law allows judges to order first-time offenders to take the drugs. If the felon doesn't voluntarily submit to chemical castration, he will be surgically castrated. In 1997, Montana became the second state to approve chemical castration. Montana law does not mandate injections but allows judges to impose them for a second offense of rape or incest. Florida passed a similar law in 1997, imposing weekly injections of Depo-Provera on paroled sex offenders. The drug is widely used as a long-acting birth control pill for women. One injection lasts about three months. Depo-Provera blocks the production of testosterone, the male hormone that generates sex drive. Effects of the drug are short term, and sex drive returns to normal once the injections stop.

Those opposed to the idea of chemical castration as punishment argue that our entire system of treating and punishing sex offenders is flawed and that we need to do more to prevent violent sex crime instead of focusing simply on punishment. The lack of effective intervention with young sex offenders is a key problem. More important, sex offenders are not always, or perhaps not even usually, driven by sex but, rather, by a desire for power or control over others. Drug treatments fail to treat the root of the problem.

Opponents also argue that the law is a serious infringement on the right to privacy, in particular the right to control one's own body and refuse unwanted medical treatments. It also constitutes "cruel and unusual punishment," prohibited under the Eighth Amendment.

In a twist on the castration theme, Ricardo José Garcia, a 37-year-old former social studies teacher in Florida, asked to be surgically castrated in exchange for a lighter prison sentence. He was accused of molesting an 11-year-old boy and if convicted would be sentenced to life in prison. The judge in the case denied Garcia's request. Another twist on the theme is the case of Larry Don McQuay, a Texas inmate who has begged the state to castrate him. He claims to have molested over 200 children and says he just can't help himself and will resume his pattern of abuse when released from prison.

Discussion Questions

1. Is chemical castration an appropriate "treatment" for sex offenders?

2. Is it a treatment or a punishment?

3. Do convicted criminals have a right to privacy, or do they forfeit this right when they commit a crime?

4. Should voluntary requests for castration be honored? In exchange for a lighter sentence?

Resources

American Civil Liberties Union. http://aclu.org (accessed July 25, 2003).

Bureau of Justice Statistics, National Crime Victimization Survey. www.ojp. usdoj.gov/bjs/ (accessed July 25, 2003).

California Penal Code. 2004. www.legalinfo.ca.gov/calaw.html (accessed June 4, 2004).

Rape, Abuse, and Incest National Network, Statistics. www.rainn.org/ statistics/ html (accessed September 9, 2003).

SPALDING, LARRY HELM. 1997. "Chemical Castration: A Return to the Dark Ages." www.aclufl.org/body_chem.html (accessed July 25, 2003).

VICARIOUS SENSITIZATION

Most adult sex offenders commit their first offense as teenagers. Add to this fact a second one—that at least half a million juveniles commit a sex crime every year—and you know we have a serious problem. Many specialized treatment programs have arisen to address this epidemic of sex offenses. Some employ a method called vicarious sensitization (VS), a kind of aversion therapy whereby the sex offender learns to associate "deviant arousal" with humiliation, pain, jail, and emotional rejection.

In VS, offenders are shown videotapes that include such vignettes as an offender molesting someone and being caught by his mother, being threatened with shooting by the victim's father, his arrest being broadcast on TV news, castration surgery being prescribed by a doctor, and similar incidents of pain or humiliation. Following is an excerpt from a VS study funded by the National Institutes of Mental Health, conducted by M. Weinrott, Ph.D.:

> . . . 69 adolescent child molesters were exposed to 300–350 VS trials over 25 sessions. . . . Youths were ages 13–18 and had offended one or more victims at least four years younger than they, and had demonstrated moderate to high levels of deviant arousal in a pre-treatment phallometric assessment. . . . Results of the phallometric assessment showed that, for most stimuli, significant decreases in arousal were obtained for youths who had received VS.
>
> — (www.northwestmedia.com/vs/summary/html)

The development of VS is seen, by the study's authors, to offer a distinct improvement over other methods of aversive conditioning, particularly electroconvulsive (shock) therapy, which is ethically problematic.

Aversion therapy does have its critics. Some have questioned the whole idea of "therapeutic punishment," arguing that therapy and punishment should remain distinct social and individual goals. Others are bothered by the notion that psychiatry is used to enforce social conformity to particular sexual norms. (Aversion therapy is still used in some cases as a therapeutic tool to convert gays into heterosexuals.) Some see aversion therapy as a form of mind control (see Anthony Burgess's *A Clockwork Orange*). And, finally, some have worried about the issue of informed consent. Are teenagers old enough to give "informed" consent to participate in a research trial on VS? Is there potential for psychological trauma, and is this potential compelling enough to advise against VS for young people?

Discussion Questions

1. Are teenagers old enough to give "informed" consent to participate in a research trial on VS?

2. In the research study reported above, voluntary written consent was obtained from all of the subjects. But where "treatment" is part of a punishment, the line between voluntary and coerced may become blurred. If VS were ordered as part of a court sentence, would it be ethically objectionable?

3. Does VS sound like "mind control"? And is "mind control" a bad thing?

4. Does the notion of "therapeutic punishment" make sense?

Resources

BURGESS, ANTHONY. 1988. *A Clockwork Orange*. New York: W. W. Norton.

LEINWAND, S. N. 1976. "Aversion Therapy: Punishment as Treatment and Treatment as Cruel and Unusual Punishment." *Southern California Law Review* 49(4): 880–983.

MATSON, J. L and T. M. DILORENZO. 1984. *Punishment and Its Alternatives*. New York: Springer.

WEINROTT, MARK R., MICHAEL RIGGAN, and STUART FROTHINGHAM. 2004. "Reducing Deviant Arousal in Juvenile Sex Offenders Using Vicarious Sensitization." Northwest Media, Inc. www.northwestmedia.com/vs/report/html (accessed June 4, 2004).

TORTURE OF A KIDNAPPER

In September 2002, Jakob von Metzler, the 11-year-old son of a prominent German banker, was abducted on his way home from school. The wealthy family readily agreed to pay the ransom money. During the hand-off, police identified their suspect. When the boy had still not been released after several days, the police made the arrest. Acting on the possibility that the boy might still be alive, the policeman questioning the kidnapper decided to do what he must to make the suspect talk, even if it meant hurting him.

As it turned out, the threat of violence was enough to make the suspect confess, and he revealed that the boy was already dead.

But the case was hardly resolved in the public's mind. Was it appropriate for the police to threaten a suspect with physical violence? Would carrying through with physical torture have been justified, had it been necessary to elicit information? Was the deviation from accepted rules of police conduct worth the possibility of saving a child's life?

Human rights advocates were appalled that the possibility of torture had even been raised. The German constitution states: "Suspects being held in police detention may not be emotionally or physically abused." Even more broadly, the United Nations Universal Declaration of Human Rights (Article 5) and the International Covenant on Civil and Political Rights (Article 7) both provide that no person "shall be subjected to torture or to cruel, inhuman or degrading treatment or punishment." Torture is defined by the United Nations as "any act by which severe pain or suffering, whether physical or mental, is intentionally inflicted on a person for such purposes as obtaining from him or a third person information or a confession" (United Nations Convention against Torture and Other Cruel, Inhuman or Degrading Treatment or Punishment, Article 1).

Discussion Questions

1. Is it ever acceptable to do something "bad" in order to reach a "good" outcome?

2. Does it matter that it was uncertain whether using torture to get information would help?

3. How immoral is threatening to torture, compared with actually torturing?

4. What if you have no intention of carrying through with the torture? What if you do?

Resources

DERSHOWITZ, ALAN M. 2003. "Threat of Torture Raises Painful Moral Questions." *Los Angeles Times*, April 21.
"Police Threat Fuels Debate on Torture." 2003. *Deutsche Welle*. www. dw-world.de/english/0,3367,1430_A_785751_1_A,00.html (accessed June 11, 2003).
United Nations, Office of the High Commissioner for Human Rights. 1987. "Convention against Torture and Other Cruel, Inhuman or Degrading Treatment or Punishment." www.unhchr.ch.html/menu3/b/h_cat39. htm (accessed July 10, 2003).

THREE NUNS AND A SILO

At dawn on October 6, 2002, with the United States poised to go to war against Iraq, three people dressed in white jumpsuits cut through a security fence at "November 8" (N-8), the Defense Department's name for the Minuteman missile site near Greeley, Colorado. Within the hour, Air Force security forces arrested the intruders at gunpoint.

As it turned out, the white jumpsuits belonged to three Roman Catholic nuns, who called themselves "disarmament specialists" and members of the Citizen Weapons Inspection Team. The nuns were engaged in symbolic disarmament: they poured their own blood, in the pattern of a holy cross, onto the missile silo and hit the lid of the concrete silo with ballpeen hammers. they did no physical damage to the missile or the silo property. October 6th marked the one-year anniversary of the U.S. invasion of Afghanistan.

The three nuns are members of the Plowshares Movement (named for the biblical injunction to "beat swords into plowshares") and were protesting the continuing nuclear armament by the U.S. government. As inspection teams were scouring Iraq looking for weapons of mass destruction, the nuns formed an internal WMD inspection team. According to the nuns, the Minuteman III is a first-strike weapon prohibited by international treaty. A Minuteman missile has an explosive power of 300 kilotons, about 20 times more powerful than the bomb dropped on Hiroshima, according to testimony at the nuns' trial from a professor of international law.

Jackie Hudson, Carol Gilbert, and Ardeth Platte were convicted of obstructing national defense and damaging government property. They were sentenced in July 2003 to prison sentences ranging from 30 to 40 months, about half as long as called for by federal sentencing guidelines. All three had previous protest-related convictions. In his statement to the nuns, U.S. District Judge Robert Blackburn called the nuns' actions "dangerously irresponsible" and said, "it's hard to find courage and honor in the violations committed by these three defendants. The courage and honor belongs to the men and women in the Air Force who protect the missiles" (*Daily Times-Call*, July 26, 2003, p. A3).

Supporters of these peace activists were disappointed with the sentences. Some argued that because the war with Iraq was imminent, the prosecution of the nuns was overly punitive and was motivated to suppress antiwar sentiment.

Discussion Questions

1. Should the nuns have been convicted of a crime and put in prison?

2. Was their punishment overly severe? Was it severe enough?

3. How should the government respond to acts of civil resistance?

4. Should the government respond differently if the country is at war?

Resources

BEDAU, HUGO ADAM, 1969. *Civil Disobedience*. New York: MacMillen.
BRENNAN, CHARLIE. 2002. "A Force of Habits: Nuns Raid Silo Site." *Rocky Mountain News*, December 4. www.commondreams.org/headlines02/1204-06.htm.
PLASKET, B. J. 2003. "Nuns Face Punishment for Defacing Missile Silo." *Daily Times-Call*, July 25, B1.
PLASKET, B. J. 2003. "Nuns Sentenced." *Daily Times-Call*, July 26, A1.

STEALING FROM THE WISHING WELL

The Trevi Fountain. It is a thing of beauty, a source of wonder and awe, and a receptacle for countless coins tossed, with whispered dreams, into the sparkling waters.

For Robert Cercelletta, the Trevi Fountain was a steady source of income. Using rake, magnet, and bare hands, Mr. Cercelletta had collected by night the coins tossed by day. In about 15 minutes, he might collect as much as $1,000, though often a great deal less. Unemployed and mentally unstable, he had been fishing the fountain for over 30 years before he was finally arrested. Although police had long known about Mr. Cercelletta, they had viewed him with amusement and had ignored his daily dips into the Trevi. Then, in 1999, a new law made it illegal to wade into city monuments like the Trevi. Mr. Cercelletta was issued a series of fines for breaking this law, all of which he ignored. Once police began monitoring Mr. Cercelletta's dips into the fountain, they realized what a large sum of money was disappearing with him.

In his own defense, Mr. Cercelletta claimed that he was not collecting very much money. What he did collect, he shared with other needy people. Anyway, he argued, if he didn't loot the fountain, someone else surely would.

Although the coins in the Trevi Fountain were nobody's property, the city collected the coins—the few that were left—once a week and donated them to various charities.

Discussion Questions

1. Assess the argument "If I didn't do it, somebody else would."

2. Assess the Robin Hood defense for stealing. Is stealing "to help those in need" justified? In what circumstances?

3. Was Robert Cercelletta a thief or an entrepreneur?

Resources

BRUNI, FRANK. 2002. "He Made a Gold Mine of the Trevi Fountain." *New York Times.* Online edition. http://travel2.nytimes.com/mem/travel/article-page.html?
STERNBACH, CLAUDIA. 2002. "Wishes Get Whisked Away." *Santa Cruz Sentinel,* Online edition. August 18. www.santacruzsentinel.com/res=950DEFDAIE3BF934A3575BCOA964968B63 archive/2002/August/18/style/stories/03style.htm.

THE CONSENTING VICTIM

Armin Meiwes, a computer specialist from Germany, testified in court that the man he stabbed and then ate had given prior consent. Meiwes said that he met his victim, Bernd Jürgen Brades, in an Internet chat room. Brades consented to being eaten. After agreeing to the plan over the Internet, the two men met at Meiwes's farmhouse, where Brades numbed himself with sleeping pills and schnapps. First, they dined together on a piece of Brades's flesh that they had sawed off and roasted. After this communal meal, they continued with the drama: Meiwes stabbed Brades to death and cut him up into pieces small enough to fit in the freezer. For the next few days, Meiwes enjoyed Brades's flesh (sometimes with red wine). Before his arrest, Meiwes was busily searching the Internet for more willing victims. In his testimony, Meiwes said that more than 200 people had answered his ad seeking a young man who wanted to be eaten. Cannibalism is not illegal in Germany, but killing on request is and carries a sentence of six months to five years. Meiwes was convicted of manslaughter and sentenced to eight and a half years in prison.

Discussion Questions

1. Assuming that Brades did indeed consent to the act, is there anything wrong with what Meiwes did? What, exactly, is the wrongdoing?

2. Can one meaningfully consent to being killed?

3. Is it murder if the "victim" has consented?

4. How would you compare this "consent to be killed" with the consent given by a terminally ill person requesting physician-assisted suicide?

5. According to court testimony, Brades was depressed. Should this have made any difference in the outcome of the case?

Resources

Associated Press. 2003. "Germany: Cannibal Defendant Sought Other Victims." *New York Times,* December 9, A6.

FLEISHMAN, JEFFREY. 2003. "Germans Get a Look at Dark Side of Cyberspace." *Los Angeles Times,* December 31, A3.

EXECUTION OF AN ABORTION-PROVIDER'S KILLER

Paul Jennings Hill, a former Presbyterian minister, was executed by the state of Florida on September 4, 2003. His crime: he shot to death an abortion doctor named Dr. Britton and his volunteer escort outside an abortion clinic in Pensacola. In his final interview before his death, Hill said, "I believe in the short and long term, more and more people will act on the principles for which I stand. . . . I'm willing and I feel very honored that they are most likely going to kill me for what I did." In an earlier interview, he had said, "The thing that kept me going through it was that I knew that if that man got into that abortion clinic, he would kill 25 to 30 people."

Most of the protestors at Hill's execution were white men, there to support his act. One supporter said that Mr. Hill had "raised the standard" for abortion protesters. Others held banners: "Dead Doctors Can't Kill," "Killing Baby Killers Is Justified Homicide," and "Extremism in Defense of Life Is Not Extreme."

Discussion Questions

1. Does the phrase "justifiable homicide" make sense?

2. Which homicides might be justifiable? (And should they still be labeled "homicide"?)

3. Hill compared the killing of an abortion doctor to the killing of Hitler. Would killing Hitler be a justified homicide? What is the difference between Hitler and Dr. Britton?

4. Does Hill deserve the death penalty?

5. Can Hill's act be seen as "civil disobedience"? Compare this case to "Three Nuns and a Silo."

Resources

GOODNOUGH, ABBY. 2003. "Florida Executes Killer of an Abortion Provider." *New York Times*, September 4, A12.

WHITE-COLLAR CRIME

Enron. Arthur Anderson. Martha Stewart and ImClone. The savings and loan scandal. Sunbeam. WorldCom. Tyco International. Price gouging of California energy companies.

Corporate malfeasance and misdeeds by the rich and powerful are so common that the daily news reports of fraud and corruption pass almost unnoticed. Perhaps we have come to accept that these things just happen and that certain bad deeds go unpunished. But some consider the polite look-the-other-way attitude toward white-collar crime a profound injustice, not only to the victims of these crimes but also to the common street criminal whose crimes are subject to the full force of the law.

Sociologist Edwin Sutherland coined the term "white-collar crime" more than 60 years ago to refer to "crime committed by a person of respectability and high social status in the course of his occupation." The definition still includes crimes committed by the rich but has expanded somewhat to encompass a whole range of crimes involving money or property: antitrust violations, bribery, bankruptcy fraud, kickbacks, insider trading, embezzlement, environmental law violations, corruption by public officials, tax evasion, and securities fraud (to name just a few). The Federal Bureau of Investigation defines white-collar crime as "those illegal acts which are characterized by deceit, concealment, or violation of trust and which are not dependent upon the application or threat of physical force or violence." (Barnett, 2003) Almost without exception, the motivation behind white-collar crime is money and what it buys: power.

White-collar crime is "nonviolent" in the sense that there is usually no direct physical harm. Yet it is often profoundly harmful. The most obvious harm, of course, is financial. Sometimes an individual can be severely damaged. An elderly woman cheated out of her pension by a con man suffers severely. Sometimes the financial harm is more diffuse: Californians paying more for their electricity than they should, taxpayers footing the bill for cleanup of Superfund sites. The cost to individual victims is small, but the total amount of money that white-collar criminals amass is enormous—often in the millions. The FBI estimates that the cost to the United States of white-collar crime amounts to more that $338 billion a year (compared to about $3.8 billion for street crime).

Although white-collar crime is less directly violent than, say, murder or kidnapping, people nevertheless may suffer physical pain and sometimes even death. One of the most famous examples of large-scale physical harm occurred when Ford Motor Company, acting on the advice of its actuaries, decided not to recall Pintos whose gas tanks exploded on impact because the cost of lawsuits for severe burn injuries (Ford's estimate: 180 lawsuits, at $67,000 each) was cheaper than the cost of fixing the problem (Ford's estimate: $11 per car).

Penalties for white-collar crime are in stark contrast to penalties for street crime. A common thief might get 40 years—perhaps even the death penalty, if he kills someone during a robbery. The white-collar criminal, in contrast, will rarely see any jail time, and if a jail sentence is handed down, it generally will be quite short (the average is 16 months) and served at a minimum-security ("country club") penitentiary. In one study comparing prison sentences, the time served by the major criminals in the savings and loan scandal—those who stole $100,000 or more—averaged about 36.4 months. Common burglars, whose take was usually less than $300, averaged 55 months. First-time drug offenders got almost 69 months (Reclaim Democracy 2001). Even the corporate executive who is (indirectly) responsible for 30 or 40 deaths may get off with nothing more than a slap on the wrist. White-collar criminals often avoid punishment altogether. President Nixon received a full pardon for his part in the Watergate scandal.

White-collar crooks can usually hire the best lawyers around and sometimes can pay someone off to "adjust" their sentence. And where there is money, there are also scapegoats and fall guys. Crimes are often committed by a corporation rather than a single individual—the guilt is spread out, often so thin as to be hard to pin down. Corporations cannot be jailed, though they can be fined.

WHITE-COLLAR CRIME, TAKE TWO: ATLANTIC STATES FOUNDRY

Five senior managers of Atlantic States, a New Jersey foundry, were indicted in December 2003 for routine violations of worker safety codes and environmental regulations. According to federal investigators, the foundry routinely dumped thousands of gallons of contaminated wastewater into the Delaware River, all the while submitting false pollution-monitoring reports. The company also repeatedly ignored safety problems that would have been expensive or bothersome to fix. One worker was killed by a forklift with a known brake problem, and another lost three fingers because a safety device had been removed from a cement mixer. Frank Wagner, who worked at a McWane factory, was killed when an industrial oven exploded, crushing him under its steel door.

According to the team of prosecutors and investigators looking into the case, Wagner's death was the direct result of criminally reckless conduct by McWane, Inc. This should have carried a charge of manslaughter for some responsible individual. But McWane was instead issued a $500,000 fine for "hazardous waste violation." A total of nine workers have died at McWane since

1995, most of these a result of safety violations or lapses. According to federal law, causing the death of a worker by willfully violating safety regulations is only a misdemeanor, which carries a maximum of six months in prison.

The motive for the repeated health and safety violations was to maximize production, and thus profit, for the company. The foundry is owned by Birmingham-based McWane Inc., the nation's largest manufacturer of cast iron pipe.

Discussion Questions

1. Is there any essential moral difference between white-collar crime and street crime? If so, what is it?

2. How different is causing a death through "willfully disregarding safety violations" from driving while drunk?

3. What would be a just punishment for the five managers at McWane?

4. Should the CEO of McWane be held responsible? What if he or she had encouraged the safety violations? What if he or she was ignorant of what lower-level managers were doing?

Resources

BARNETT, CYNTHIA. 2003. "The Measurement of White-Collar Crime Using Uniform Crime Reporting (UCR) Data." U.S. Department of Justice, Federal Bureau of Investigation, Criminal Justice Information Services Division.

BARSTOW, DAVID. 2003. "Officials at Foundry Face Health and Safety Charges." *New York Times*, December 16, A22.

BARSTOW, DAVID, and LOWELL BERGMAN. 2003. "Deaths on the Job, Slaps on the Wrist." *New York Times*, January 10. www.coastal.edu/ bob/Deaths%20 on %20 the %20Job.html. (accessed December 17, 2003).

FRIEDRICHS, DAVID. O. 1995. *Trusted Criminals: White Collar Crime in Contemporary Society.* Belmont, CA: Wadsworth.

LEAF, CLIFTON. 2002. "Enough Is Enough: They Lie They Cheat They Steal and They've Been Getting Away with It for Too Long." *Fortune*, March 18.

NADER, RALPH. 1991. *Unsafe at Any Speed.* New York: Knightsbridge.

Public Broadcasting Service. 2003. "Frontline: A Dangerous Business." Aired on January 9, 2003. Produced by Neil Docherty and David Rummel, reported by David Barstow and Lowell Bergman, written by Lowell Bergman, David Rummel, and Linden MacIntye. Transcript at www.pbs.org/wgbh/pages/frontline/shows/workplace/etc/script. html (accessed December 17, 2003).

Reclaim Democracy. 2001. "Killing for Capital: Corporate Crime and the Dual Standard of Justice." www.ReclaimDemocracy.org (accessed December 10, 2003).

REIMAN, H. JEFFREY. 2004. *The Rich Get Richer and the Poor Get Prison: Ideology, Class, and Criminal Justice.* 3rd ed. New York: Allyn & Bacon.

ROSOFF, STEPHEN M., HENRY N. PONTELL, and ROBERT TILLMAN. 2001. *Profit Without Honor: White Collar Crime and the Looting of America.* 2nd ed. Englewood Cliffs, NJ: Prentice Hall.

WIESBURD, DAVID. 2001. *White-Collar Crime and Criminal Careers.* Cambridge: Cambridge University Press.

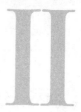

Life and *Death*

Elder Suicide or Dignified Exit? A Letter from Ohio

Fetal Rights and the Fetus as Person: The Case of J.D.S.

Fetal Rights, Take Two: Unborn Victims of Violence Act

Fetal Rights, Take Three: Drug Abuse and Fetal Abuse

Zero Population Growth

Suicide Concert

Growth Hormones for Shortness

Age-Based Cost Studies

Medical Care for Prisoners

Medical Care for Prisoners, Take Two: Donor Heart Goes to a Criminal

Medical Care for Prisoners, Take Three: Organ Transplant for Death Row Inmate

Fetal Testing for Down Syndrome

Age-Extension Research

The Schiavos

ELDER SUICIDE OR DIGNIFIED EXIT? A LETTER FROM OHIO

I'm 80. I've had a good life—mostly pretty happy, though certainly with its ups and downs. My wife died seven years ago. My children are healthy and happy, busy with their kids, careers, friends. But I know they worry about me; they feel increasingly burdened with thoughts about how to care for me when I can no longer care for myself, which—let's not kid ourselves—is coming all too soon. I live four states away from them so either they will have to uproot me and move me close to them or I'll have to go live in a nursing home. I don't relish either option. This town has been my home for nearly my whole adult life, and I don't fancy leaving. On the other hand, I do not want to live among strangers and be cared for by those who are paid minimum wage to wash urine-soaked sheets and force-feed pudding to old people.

I'm in decent health—for the moment. But things are slipping. I have prostrate cancer, like just about every other man my age. It probably won't kill me . . . but having to get up and pee four or five times a night, standing over the bowl for long minutes just hoping something will come out, this might do me in. My joints are stiff, so it doesn't really feel good to walk. I've got bits and pieces of skin cancer here and there that need to be removed. These things are all "treatable," or so they say (there are pills to take and procedures to have done). But it seems to me a waste of money. Why not pass my small savings on to my grandkids, to give them a jump on college tuition?

What I don't understand is why people think that it is wrong for someone like me to just call it a day, throw in the towel. How can it be possible that I don't have a "right" to end my own life, when I'm ready? (But apparently I don't.)

I'm tired and I'm ready to be done with life. I'd so much rather just quietly die in my garage with the car running than eke out these last few compromised years. (Even better would be a quick shot or a small dose of powerful pills—but, alas, these are not at my disposal.)

But if I do myself in, I will be called a "suicide." My death will be added to the statistics: another "elder suicide." How sad!

(Doesn't the fact that so many elderly people commit suicide—and with much greater rates of success, I must say, than any other demographic group—doesn't this tell you something?) Why can't this society just come up with a humane, acceptable plan for those of us ready to be finished? Why can't we old folks go to city hall and pick up our End-of-Life Packet, with the financial and legal forms to bring things into order for our children, with assistance on how to recycle all our unneeded furniture and clothes, and with a neat little pack of white pills: When ready, take all 10 pills at once, with plenty of water. Lie down quietly in a comfortable place, close your eyes, and wait.

How can choosing my own end at my own time be considered anything other than a most dignified final exit?

— Anonymous. June, 2003

Discussion Questions

1. Should people have the moral right to end their lives, if they so please?

2. Does being near the end of one's life make the decision to end it justified?

3. What might the phrase "right to die" mean?

4. Do people have the right to seek assistance in dying?

5. Do people have the right to give assistance in dying?

6. What kind of restrictions, if any, should there be on assisted suicide?

Resources

CLARKE, D. M. 1999. "Autonomy, Rationality, and the Wish to Die." *Journal of Medical Ethics* 25, no. 6 (December): 457–62.

HUMPHREY, DEREK. 2002. *Final Exit: The Practicalities of Self-Deliverance and Assisted Suicide for the Dying.* 3rd ed. New York: Delta Trade Paperbacks.

LESTER, DAVID, and MARGOT TALLMER, eds. 1994. *Now I Lay Me Down: Suicide in the Elderly.* Philadelphia: Charles Press.

MCINTOSH, JOHN L., JOHN F. SANTOS, and RICHARD W. HUBBARD. 1994. *Elder Suicide: Research, Theory, and Treatment.* Washington, DC: American Psychological Association.

OCHSHORN, EZRA. 2003. "Elder Suicide: Are You Aware of It?" *Christian Science Monitor*, June 2. www.csmonitor.com/2003/0602/p11s02-coop.html (accessed December 10, 2003).

QUILL, TIMOTHY E. 1994. *Death and Dignity: Making Choices and Taking Charge.* New York: W. W. Norton.

SALVATORE, T. 2000. "Elder Suicide: A Preventable Tragedy." *Caring* 19, no. 3 (March): 34–37.

STONE, GEO. 2001. *Suicide and Attempted Suicide: Methods and Consequences.* New York: Carroll and Graf.

FETAL RIGHTS AND THE FETUS AS PERSON: THE CASE OF J.D.S.

She weighs 88 pounds; she has seizures, cerebral palsy, and autism; she has the mental capacity of a young child. She cannot speak—cannot say who raped her in the state-run group home where she lives. But someone did, because she is pregnant.

A guardian was appointed to make medical decisions for J.D.S. during her pregnancy—common practice when a patient is considered incompetent to make her own medical decisions. But state lawyers in Florida, dispatched by Governor Jeb Bush, tried to go a step further and appoint a separate guardian for J.D.S.'s fetus. According to an assistant state attorney general, J.D.S.'s guardian would not necessarily make decisions in the best interest of the fetus. The American Civil Liberties Union and other groups filed an amicus brief asking that the state deny requests for a separate guardian.

The question of whether or not J.D.S.'s fetus should have a guardian is now moot: J.D.S is nine months pregnant, and late-term abortion is illegal in Florida. But her case has become a focal point for fierce debate over the issues of abortion and of so-called fetal rights. Both anti-abortion and pro-choice groups see this case as an attempt to move toward restrictions on abortion by establishing legal protection for fetuses.

Abortion rights groups, who were allowed to present arguments in court, argued that appointing a guardian would establish that fetuses were "persons." This would then imply that fetuses could be protected even from pregnant women themselves. And this looks to pro-choice people like a serious intrusion into the private lives of pregnant women.

FETAL RIGHTS, TAKE TWO: UNBORN VICTIMS OF VIOLENCE ACT

In April 2001, the House of Representatives approved (for the second time) a bill that would criminalize harm to a fetus in connection with a felony crime committed against the mother. The Unborn Victims of Violence Act would make it a separate felony to harm an unborn child in the course of committing any one of the 68 federal felony offenses. H.R. 503 classifies a fertilized egg, zygote, blastocyst, embryo, or fetus as a separate entity for the purpose of federal law. The bill now before the Senate, S. 146 makes it a separate crime to cause injury or death to a child who is in utero at the time the conduct takes place. "The terms 'child in utero' and 'child, who is in utero' mean a member of the species *Homo sapiens,* at any stage of development, who is carried in the womb." The bill does not allow prosecution for legal abortion or for conduct of a woman with respect to her own unborn child. The murder of Laci Peterson (eight months pregnant) and her unborn son, Connor, has fueled support for the passage of the Unborn Victims of Violence Act in the Senate.

President Bush supports the legislation, saying it "affirms our commitment to a culture of life, which welcomes and protects children." Passage of the bill is strongly supported by the National Right to Life Committee and other pro-life groups. The legislation is opposed by Planned Parenthood, National Abortion and Reproductive Rights Action League, and other abortion rights groups, even though the bill explicitly excludes abortion. It is also opposed by the American Civil Liberties Union because it sees the bill as an attempt to undermine reproductive freedom. The bill does not define the fetus as a "person" but only as a "victim" of crime. Nevertheless, it does endow a fetus with legal rights distinct from those of the pregnant woman.

As of April 2003, 26 states have enacted laws that recognize the unborn child as a separate victim of violent crime. Fifteen states have homicide laws that recognize the child in utero as victim during any stage of development; thirteen states provide protection during later stages of fetal development.

FETAL RIGHTS, TAKE THREE: DRUG ABUSE AND FETAL ABUSE

Regina McKnight, a South Carolina woman who gave birth to a stillborn child, is being prosecuted for homicide by child abuse. She is accused of murdering her unborn child through using cocaine. If convicted, she could face up to 20 years in prison.

Discussion Questions

1. If a fetus is considered a "person," does it follow that the fetus has the full range of "rights" to which an already-born person is entitled? (What makes any person *entitled* to rights?)

2. What kind of "rights," if any, might a fetus have?

3. Would these rights trump the rights of a pregnant woman?

4. How would one compare abortion with criminal treatment of third-party killings of fetuses?

5. How should one compare abortion policies with policies toward pregnant women who abuse drugs?

6. Does the fetus of a pregnant woman who smokes or drinks need protection? What kind of protection, if any, would be justified?

7. Judges in Florida worried that if J.D.S.'s fetus deserved protection, then the state would need to appoint guardians for many other fetuses, too. If J.D.S.'s fetus were granted a guardian, would this imply that fetuses of women who abuse drugs or alcohol also deserve protection, or are the cases different in significant ways?

Resources

FLETCHER, JOSEPH. 1979. *Humanhood: Essays in Biomedical Ethics*. Buffalo, NY: Prometheus Books.

GOODNOUGH, ABBY. 2003. "Guardian Sought for Fetus of a Retarded Floridian." *New York Times*, August 22, A14.

JANSSEN, N. D. 2000. "Fetal Rights and the Prosecution of Women for Using Drugs During Pregnancy." *Drake Law Review* 48 (4): 741–68.

MARRUS, E. 2002. "Crack Babies and the Constitution: Ruminations about Addicted Pregnant Women after *Ferguson v. City of Charleston.*" *Villanova Law Review* 47 (2): 299–340.

National Right to Life Committee. 2003. "State Homicide Laws That Recognize Unborn Victims." www.nrlc.org/Unborn_Victims/Statehomicidelaws092302.html (accessed August 29, 2003).

SCHROEDEL, JEAN REITH. 2000. "'Is the Fetus a Person?' A Comparison of Policies across the Fifty States." *New England Journal of Medicine*, December 7.

ZERO POPULATION GROWTH

For most of the time that humans have inhabited the earth, our numbers have grown slowly. We reached our first billion only at the beginning of the 19th century. But during the 20th century, human numbers surged in a steep upward curve of growth. At the turn of the 21st century, the U.S. Census Bureau population clock read about 6.25 billion. Although the fertility rate has been declining for the past 30 years, the world adds about 75 million people each year. Modest estimates by the United Nations project a population of at least 9 billion by 2050.

Whether or not these numbers represent a problem has been under intense debate since at least the 1960s, when environmental decline became a serious concern. Many demographers and public health researchers consider the surging numbers of humans to be the most pressing problem currently facing humanity and the cornerstone of a potential catastrophe.

The problem, as the worriers see it, is not simply an increase in number of humans but, rather, an increase in numbers coupled with a rapid intensification of human industrial activity. During the past century, aggregate global production and consumption curves rose even more sharply than population. While population quadrupled, the overall global economy grew by a factor of 14, energy use by 16, carbon dioxide emissions by 17, and industrial output by 40 (McNeill 2001). Since more energy, more raw material, more sinks for pollution simply cannot be created, we must recognize that there are limits to growth.

The best way to offset environmental decline is to reduce consumption and slow growth simultaneously. A number of international organizations and governments are working to slow growth, including the United Nations Population Programme and the World Health Organization. Grassroots citizen groups have also been organized in the United States and elsewhere around the world. One of the key activist groups in the United States is called Population Connection (formerly Zero Population Growth). Here is an excerpt from their statement of goals:

> As a U.S. based organization, Population Connection works primarily to educate and motivate Americans to help meet the global population challenge, and to mobilize this support for the adoption of policies and programs necessary to slow population growth. Because the United States is the chief consumer of the world's resources, slowing its population growth is disproportionately important for protecting the global environment. Because the United States has a major influence on international political, economic and military affairs, reshaping its policies is important for the success of international efforts to slow population growth.
>
> — (Population Connection 2003)

These are some of the specific objectives stated by Population Connection:

- Expansion of family planning services throughout the United States and the world. The developed nations should provide funding to the developing nations.
- Universal access to family planning and abortion services in the United States.
- Removal of existing state restrictions on contraceptive availability for teenagers.
- Broad dissemination of information about contraception.
- Lifting of all restrictions on obtaining sterilization for adults and dissemination of information about sterilization.
- Increased federal funding of contraceptive research.

- Access for all women to medically safe and affordable abortion (including Medicaid coverage of the procedure).
- Hospitals receiving public funds must make abortion services available.
- Foreign aid should be given to fund abortion services in any country desiring such assistance.

Discussion Questions

1. How might someone who is morally opposed to abortion respond to the issue of global overpopulation?

2. Is there any moral problem with making contraceptives widely available in our own country?

3. Examine Population Connection's list of objectives. Are there any morally problematic objectives? If so, which ones are they? Why?

4. On his first day in office, President Bush imposed what is called the "Global Gag Rule" policy. This policy denies family planning funds to any international organization that uses its funds to pay for abortion services, counseling, or education. Is this an appropriate international stance on population growth?

Resources

BROWN, LESTER R., GARY GARDNER, and BRIAN HALWEIL. 1998. *Beyond Malthus: Sixteen Dimensions of the Population Problem.* Edited by Linda Starke. Worldwatch Paper No. 143. Washington, DC: Worldwatch Institute.

ELLIOT, HERSCHEL. 2002. *A General Statement of the Tragedy of the Commons* 1997. www.dieoff.com (accessed September 17, 2003).

McNEILL, JOHN R. 2001. *Something New under the Sun: An Environmental History of the Twentieth-Century World.* New York: W. W. Norton.

Population Connection. 2003. "Statement of Policy." www.populationconnection.org/About_Us/policies (accessed August 30, 2003).

SPEIDEL, JOSEPH. 2000. "Environment and Health: 1. Population, Consumption and Human Health." *Canadian Medical Association Journal* 163 (5): 551–56.

United Nations. 1999. *World Population Prospects: The 1998 Revision.* New York: United Nations.

United Nations Development Programme, United Nations Environment Programme, World Bank, and World Resources Institute. 2000. *A Guide to World Resources 2000–2001: People and Ecosystems, The Fraying Web of Life.* Washington, DC: World Resources Institute.

United Nations Population Fund. 2002. *The State of the World's Population 2001.* www.unfpa.org/swp/2001 (accessed May 5, 2002).

SUICIDE CONCERT

Hell on Earth planned a most unusual concert event. The Tampa, Florida, rock band would stage a suicide for the audience—yes, a real suicide. According to the leader of the band, Billy Tourtelot, the event was intended to raise awareness of and support for physician-assisted suicide. The suicide would be carried out by an unnamed man who claimed to be terminally ill. The St. Petersburg City Council passed an emergency ordinance declaring it illegal to sell tickets for a suicide or to conduct a suicide for commercial purposes.

Discussion Questions

1. Is suicide unethical?

2. Why is the idea of a public suicide upsetting to people?

Resources

Associated Press. 2003. "Florida: Band Promises Suicide Concert. "*New York Times,* September 30, A20.
JOHNSON, CARRIE. 2003. "Suicide Concert Is a No Show." *St. Petersburg Times,* October 5. wwwsptimes.com/2003/10/05/Tampabay/ Suicide_ concert_is_a.shtml (accessed November 17, 2003).

GROWTH HORMONES FOR SHORTNESS

Human growth hormone (hGH), which is produced by the pituitary gland, stimulates a vast number of metabolic processes that control longitudinal growth in humans. It modulates lipid, protein, and carbohydrate metabolism, and it stimulates the development of bone, cartilage, skeletal muscle, and gonadal tissue. Children with an hGH deficiency—or who have a pathology such as Turner's syndrome, which interferes with production of hGH—wind up being quite short as adults. Yet the majority of children seen by pediatric endocrinologists because of concerns about shortness have no pathology. Their parents are short, or they may have what is called idiopathic short stature (ISS)—no one knows why they do not grow as tall as other children. They simply don't. "Short stature" is defined, medically, as a height for a given age and gender that is 2 or more standard deviations below normal. Approximately 2.5 percent of children in the United States have short stature.

The first treatments for shortness—with injections of hGH derived from the brains of cadavers—took place in the late 1960s. The treatment seemed to work—the children gained an inch or two of height. But the hGH was very difficult to obtain. It took thousands of dead brain cells to extract just a few drops of hGH. Then, in the 1980s, hGH was taken off the market because it was found to cause Creutzfeld-Jacob disease (which causes fatal degeneration of the central nervous system). Thus began the search for a synthetic form of growth hormone.

The task of reproducing hGH synthetically was challenging—hGH is a protein chain of 191 amino acids that first had to be identified and then replicated. In 1985, Genentech released the first synthetic form of hGH—called Protopin. The amino acid sequence was one off, but the drug still worked. In 1986, Eli Lilly produced a synthetic version that was identical to a growth hormone of pituitary origin and called it Humatrope. Humatrope (or somatropin) is a recombinant growth hormone (derived from recombinant DNA, or rDNA) grown in a vat of genetically altered *Escherichia coli* bacteria. The supply is essentially limitless.

Recombinant growth hormone, or rhGH, has been approved by the Food and Drug Administration for a variety of pathologies leading to short stature: growth hormone deficiency, Turner's syndrome, chronic renal insufficiency, and Prader-Willi syndrome. In July 2003, the FDA went a step further—and a step too far, according to some critics—by approving the use of Humatrope for idiopathic short stature. Treatment is approved only for the shortest of the short: those children 2.25 or more standard deviations below the mean, or the shortest 1.2 percent of children.

This has generated lively debate about whether or not the drug should be given to children with ISS—where the treatment is essentially cosmetic, not medical. rhGH appears to be safe and to have only modest short-term side effects. Still, some bioethicists worry about the effects of rhGH treatment on onset of puberty and maturation of the bones. Treatment is usually effective—a sustained course of rhGH will offer a child an average increase of about an inch and a half in height. Although the costs of rhGH vary, estimates place the cost at about $20,000 a year for the four to five years of treatment. Treatment involves six injections a week. Since Humatrope has been on the market for just over 15 years, the long-term effects of using the drug are unknown.

Some bioethicists worry that if Humatrope is approved for cosmetic treatment, it will be hard to enforce restrictions on exactly who can take the drug. Although it may be indicated for the very, very short, it will be almost impossible to keep the drug out of the hands of parents whose children are just shorter than desired. This is particularly troublesome because the child (being too young) cannot give informed consent to the treatment—it will essentially be decided by the parents. The drug is expensive, and since its use is unlikely to be covered by health insurance, those who can take advantage of Humatrope will be the wealthy elite.

Furthermore, a daily injection is painful and traumatic for the child. Cosmetic use of Humatrope has larger social implications, too: By allowing the drug to be used for cosmetic purposes, we legitimate the use of medicine to alter a person's physical appearance. Supporters of cosmetic use of the drug cite a 1996 study that found that 40 percent of prescriptions for Humatrope were already for cosmetic, or "off-label" (not FDA approved), uses—so this is obviously a drug treatment in high demand.

Eli Lilly has told the FDA that it will not engage in direct-to-consumer marketing. Yet Eli Lilly does try to make its medicine appealing to children. The Humatrope Web site offers a special Safari Club, "where the fun is growing!" If you become a Humatrooper, you can get a backpack, a Humatrooper calendar, and other fun Safari Club items.

Discussion Questions

1. Should parents be the ones to decide whether children with ISS should be treated? Can children give meaningful consent to a treatment of this sort?

2. Is shortness a disability? A disadvantage?

3. Should medicines be used to address social disadvantages?

4. To what extent is it a problem that the children undergoing treatment for ISS are too young to give informed consent?

Resources

ALLEN, D. B., and N. C. FOST. 1990. "Growth Hormone for Short Stature." *Journal of Pediatric Surgery* 117, no. 1 (July): 16–21.

DIEKMA, DOUGLAS. 1990. "Is Taller Really Better? Growth Hormone Therapy in Short Children." *Perspectives in Biology and Medicine* 34, no. 1 (Autumn): 109–23.

ELLIOTT, CARL. 2003. *Better Than Well: American Medicine Meets the American Dream.* New York: W. W. Norton.

Food and Drug Administration. 2003. "FDA Approves Humatrope for Short Stature." July 25. www.fda.gov/bbs/topics/ANSWERS/2003/ANS01242.html (accessed November 19, 2003).

GRUMBACH, MELVIN. 1988. "Growth Hormone Therapy and the Short End of the Stick." *New England Journal of Medicine* 319, no. 4 (July): 238–41.

Health Technology Advisory Committee. 2000. "The Use of Human Growth Hormone for Children with Idiopathic Short Stature." February. www.health.state.mn.us/htac/hgh.htm (accessed November 18, 2003).

Humatrope Web site. www.humatrope.com/.

AGE-BASED COST STUDIES

How much is a human life worth? Is a healthy young person worth more to society than an elderly person? Apparently so. At least that is what the government says—or said, until it came under intense fire from older Americans.

The government often uses cost-benefit analysis to make regulatory decisions. For example, the costs of regulating pollution are weighed against the potential benefits to health—basically, the number of lives saved by the pollution-control measures. In most analyses all lives are worth the same, however much that might be in dollar terms. Yet the Environmental Protection Agency (EPA), under a broader administration policy, used what is called a "discounting" method in two environmental studies aimed at setting pollution regulations. The life of a person younger than 70 was valued at $3.7 million, while the life of a person older than 70 was worth $2.3 million. (Although most price have increased with inflation over the past two decades, the price of human life has dropped substantially. In the Bush administration of the early 1990s, each life was worth $6 million.)

Older citizens were duly upset at what they called the "senior death discount." What, they argued, made their lives less worthwhile than anyone else's? And if you say that old people are worth less, perhaps because they contribute less to society, what will happen to people with disabilities or those who are chronically ill? Environmental groups also criticized the studies, which they claimed were an attempt to weaken pollution regulations by decreasing the value of lives saved.

Those defending age-based cost studies argue that policies most strongly protecting the young add the most years of life to the overall calculus of benefits.

Discussion Questions

1. Can the EPA's policy be justified on moral grounds?

2. Are the lives of older people worth less than the lives of younger people?

3. Or should all lives be valued exactly the same for public policy decisions?

4. Do younger people have a right to make value judgments about the aged?

Resources

HAHN, ROBERT, and SCOTT WALLSTEN. 2003. "Whose Life Is Worth More? (And Why Is It Horrible to Ask?)." *Washingtonpost.com*, June 1. www.washingtonpost.com/ac2/wp-dyn/A60459-2003May30 (accessed July 10, 2003).

Office of Management and Budget. "Draft 2003 Report to Congress on the Costs and Benefits of Federal Regulations; Notice." *Federal Register* 68, no. 22 (February): 92–99.

OMB Watch. 2003. "Administration Devalues the Elderly." www. ombwatch.org/article/articleview/1385/ (accessed July 10, 2003).

SEELYE, KATHERINE Q., and JOHN TIERNEY. 2003. "E.P.A. Drops Age-Based Cost Studies." *New York Times,* May 8. A26.

MEDICAL CARE FOR PRISONERS

It is one of America's glaring embarrassments: millions of its citizens lack even the most basic medical care. And many more cannot afford more expensive care that would improve their quality of life. Yet commit a serious crime, and you are likely to get most of the medical care you need—all paid for by taxpayers. Inmates receive dialysis (at approximately $50,000 a year, per inmate), bone marrow transplants (somewhere between $100,000 and $200,000), HIV/AIDS drug "cocktails," along with much more routine care such as dental checkups, antidepressants, and blood pressure pills.

Medical care for prisoners is guaranteed by the Constitution, according to the Supreme Court 1976 ruling in *Estelle v. Gamble.* The Court ruled that prisoners are entitled to medical and dental care that conforms to accepted community standards. To deny them needed care is in violation of the "cruel and unusual punishment" clause of the Eighth Amendment.

Of course, not everyone believes that the medical care received by prisoners is good, much less adequate. Indeed, various studies of the health of prisoners belie the arguments that prisoners receive more than they deserve. Hepatitis is epidemic, as is AIDS, in prisons. And some reports suggest that prison health care is less than ideal. Nevertheless, cases of prisoners receiving expensive care attract national attention.

MEDICAL CARE FOR PRISONERS, TAKE TWO: DONOR HEART GOES TO A CRIMINAL

Two men share a hospital room at Stanford Medical Center. Both are desperately ill and are on a waiting list for a donor heart. Both have type B+ blood and so will be competing for the same compatible donor's heart. One man, Mike, has been waiting 68 days, but when a matching heart becomes available, Mike is recuperating from another surgery needed to keep him alive until he can have a heart. So the donor heart goes instead to his roommate—call him Bob. Bob, 31, is a convicted felon, imprisoned for two armed robberies. He suffers from a viral infection that has weakened his heart valves.

Many of those who heard about this situation were angered that Bob received the heart instead of Mike. "Why should society give a perfectly good resource to someone who doesn't deserve it? Bob has told society that he doesn't want to play by the rules, so he should be left out of the benefits, too." Mike himself, however, was unperturbed. In his view, Bob had a medical need—which was the sole criterion that mattered. Mike got his own donor heart a few weeks later.

Beyond the issue of who deserved to get the organ, the cost of Bob's transplant—about $1 million—irked many citizens, who feel that society should not foot the medical bills of criminals.

MEDICAL CARE FOR PRISONERS, TAKE THREE: ORGAN TRANSPLANT FOR DEATH ROW INMATE

Horacio Alberto Reyes-Camarena was sentenced to death in 1996 for stabbing to death an 18-year-old girl and nearly killing her older sister, who survived 17 stab wounds. While on death row, the Oregon inmate's kidney began to fail, so his correctional institution began to provide lifesaving dialysis treatment, three times a week for four hours each time. It is understandable that Reyes-Camarena would like to be free of the tedious dialysis session; he would like to have a new kidney. Since his dialysis costs the state about $120,000 a year, the transplant operation might even save taxpayers some money.

Yet the idea of giving this lifesaving treatment to a convicted killer seems wrong to many people. Kidneys are a scarce resource—almost 60,000 Americans are waiting for a kidney transplant. Budget cuts in Oregon have meant that some poor and uninsured patients have been removed from waiting lists for transplantable organs. To some people, it seems unfair for the state to finance the medical care of a convicted criminal, while the poor are sentenced to death.

However, perhaps all people in need of an organ should be treated the same. After all, if we were to base organ allocation on "deservingness," we would be hard-pressed to judge who, among law-abiding citizens, should top the list. Although early allocation systems depended to some degree on judgments about deservingness, these were roundly criticized as biased and unfair. The United Network for Organ Sharing (UNOS) says,

> Punitive attitudes that completely exclude those convicted of crimes from receiving medical treatment, including an organ transplant, are not ethically legitimate. . . .
>
> [C]onvicted criminal status should be irrelevant in the evaluation for candidacy as a potential transplant recipient. This position assumes that convicted criminals have been sentenced only to a specific punishment, i.e., incarceration, fines, or probation. However, the convicted criminal has not been sentenced by society to an additional punishment of an inability to receive consideration for medical services."
>
> — (United Network for Organ Sharing 2003)

If he had been given the kidney, Reyes-Camarena would have been Oregon's first inmate to receive a taxpayer-financed transplant. As it turned out, he did not receive the transplant because he failed certain eligibility requirements based on his medical condition.

Discussion Questions

1. Does a convicted criminal deserve whatever treatment he or she requests? Whatever is medically indicated?

2. Is a convict entitled to the same medical treatment as anyone else?

3. Should the severity of the crime determine what level of medical care a criminal receives?

4. Should law-abiding citizens be prioritized over convicted criminals when the allocation of organs for transplantation is being determined?

5. What kind of problems would be raised by using social criteria for allocating scarce resources such as donor organs?

Resources

Estelle v. Gamble, 429 U.S. 97 (1976).

GUSTAFSON, ALAN. 2003. "Death Row Inmate Seeks Organ Transplant." *StatesmanJournal.com,* Salem, Oregon. http://online.statesmanjournal. com/sp_section_article.cfm?i=59752&s=2242 (accessed December 3, 2003).

GUSTAFSON, ALAN. 2003. "Inmate Care Contrasts with Cuts in State Health Services." *StatesmanJournal.com,* Salem, Oregon. http://online. statesmanjournal.com/sp_section_article.cfm?i=59752&s=2242 (accessed December 3, 2003).

HYLTON, WIL S. 2003. "Sick on the Inside: Correctional HMOs and the Coming Prison Plague." *Harper's Magazine,* August, 43–54.

KAHN, JEFFREY. 2003. "Prisoners and Transplants." www. bioethics. umn. edu/publications/emarchive/2002.02.04%20prisoner%20trans.html (accessed December 3, 2003).

United Network for Organ Sharing. 2003. "UNOS Ethics Committee Position Statement Regarding Convicted Criminals and Transplant Evaluation." www.unos.org/resources/bioethics.asp?index=2 (accessed December 3, 2003).

FETAL TESTING FOR DOWN SYNDROME

Down syndrome, or trisomy 21, is a genetic disorder marked by three copies of chromosome 21 rather than two—hence the term "trisomy." It is most often caused by an error (a nondisjunction) during cell division. Down syndrome is the most common genetic disorder of humans and the most common genetic cause of mental retardation. It is associated with a whole spectrum of congenital malformations, including flat facial profile, small ears, an unusually large tongue, loose skin on the back of the neck, epicanthal folds at the corners of the eyes, and an upward slant to the eyes. Mental retardation can range from very mild to severe. Approximately 1 in every 800 to 1,000 children in the United States will be born with Down syndrome.

Over the past several decades, medical advances have made available techniques to test fetuses in the womb for genetic disorders such as Down syndrome. By now, almost all pregnant women receiving regular prenatal care are given what is known as the "triple screen" test. The main purpose of the triple screen is to flag pregnancies that have a high likelihood of a genetic abnormality—in particular, to test for Down syndrome.

Between the 15th and 18th weeks of pregnancy, the mother's blood is tested for alpha-fetoprotein, unconjugated estriol, and human chorionic gonadotropin. From the results of the triple screen, doctors can calculate a risk factor for Down syndrome. This calculated risk factor is then used to calculate a statistical risk based on the mother's age (the chance of having a child with Down syndrome increases the older a woman is, particularly after the age of 35). The triple screen detects about 60 percent of the pregnancies affected by trisomy 21 and has a 5 percent rate of false positives (tests that falsely indicate the presence of trisomy). A "positive" (or abnormal) triple screen does not mean that the child will have trisomy 21; the chance that a positive result is actually a trisomy is only about 2 percent. To complicate things further, some women who have a normal triple screen may still give birth to a child with Down syndrome.

If the triple screen results are positive, or if a pregnancy is considered at high risk for Down syndrome because the woman is over 35, doctors will recommend that the mother undergo amniocentesis or chorionic villus sampling (CVS). Both of these procedures are invasive and pose some risk that the fetus will be harmed, but they provide a more rigorous assessment of the likelihood of trisomy 21. During amniocentesis, a needle is inserted into the uterus, through the mother's abdomen. A small amount of amniotic fluid is removed and then tested for chromosomal abnormalities. Amniocentesis is usually done between the 14th and 18th weeks of pregnancy and carries a 2 to 3 percent risk of causing a miscarriage. In CVS, a small amount of tissue is removed from the chorionic or fetal layer of the placenta. This tissue contains fetal chromosomes, which can be tested for abnormalities. With CVS, which is carried out between the 10th and 12th weeks of pregnancy, the risk of miscarriage is 3 to 5 percent. The current recommendation is that women with a calculated risk of 1 in 250 of having a child with Down syndrome get amniocentesis or CVS.

When amniocentesis or CVS reveals a fetal trisomy 21, the parents are faced with an anguishing choice: carry the child to term and raise the child themselves, carry the child to term and put him or her up for adoption, or terminate the pregnancy. About 75 percent of trisomy 21 pregnancies will spontaneously abort, leaving another 25 percent that will live to full term if not aborted. Once born, most people with Down syndrome can live a full, if somewhat short, life. However, a number of diseases appear to occur with increased frequency in persons with trisomy 21: congenital heart disease, epilepsy, early Alzheimer's disease, and hearing loss.

Organizations like the National Down Syndrome Society (NDSS) try to raise awareness about the disorder and argue the need for increased acceptance of and sensitivity to it. Because medical treatments for people with Down syndrome are improving, the mortality rate is dropping. In the past, people with Down syndrome were lucky to live to age 9; now the average lifespan is 55. Also, more and more women are waiting until they are older to begin childbearing, another reason for an anticipated increase in the number of Down syndrome births. We can expect more and more people with Down syndrome to be a part of our lives.

The NDSS emphasizes that people with Down syndrome can be well-integrated into families and into society. People with Down syndrome are gentle and loving and have immense potential to live happy, fulfilled lives. Families report that raising a Down syndrome child can be one of life's most rewarding experiences.

Some people refuse prenatal screening for genetic disorders. They feel certain that they will carry their pregnancy to term, whatever the child's potential, and would rather not have advance knowledge of a disorder. Since amniocentesis and CVS carry a small risk of miscarriage, they feel there is no reason for them to have the testing done. Others request the tests, even though they have no intention of terminating the pregnancy if a genetic disorder is detected. They believe that knowing in advance that they are going to have a child with Down syndrome will allow them the opportunity to become educated about the disorder, to get prepared emotionally and financially, to prepare siblings for the experience, and so forth.

Still, many people do not feel up to the emotional or financial challenge of raising a child with special needs. These people may seriously consider terminating a pregnancy when amniocentesis or CVS indicates the presence of trisomy 21.

Discussion Questions

1. Would it be wrong for parents to abort a fetus with trisomy 21?

2. Tay-Sachs is a severe genetic disorder in which harmful amounts of a substance called ganglioside GMS accumulate in the brain. Although a Tay-Sachs infant will appear normal for the first few months, a rapid process of deterioration soon sets in, causing blindness, deafness, an inability to swallow, muscle atrophy, and finally, sometime before age 5, death. Is there a moral difference between

choosing to abort a fetus with trisomy 21 and a fetus with Tay-Sachs disease?

3. Are there any circumstances that would justify aborting a child with Down syndrome?

4. What are the strengths of the argument that any kind of prenatal testing is wrong?

Resources

KUHSE, HELGA, and PETER SINGER. 1985. *Should the Baby Live? The Problem of Handicapped Newborns*. New York: Oxford University Press.
LESHIN, LEN. 1998–2002. "Prenatal Screening for Down Syndrome." www.ds-health.com/prenatal.htm (accessed November 25, 2003).
National Down Syndrome Society. www.ndss.org (accessed November 25, 2003).
National Institutes of Child Health and Human Development. 2003. "Facts about Down Syndrome" (No. 97-3402). www.nichd. nih.gov/publications/pubs/downsyndrome/down.htm (accessed December 5, 2003).
NEWBERGER, DAVID S. 2000. "Down Syndrome: Prenatal Risk Assessment and Diagnosis." *American Family Physician*, August 15.

AGE-EXTENSION RESEARCH

The President's Council on Bioethics released a lengthy report in October 2003 called *Beyond Therapy*. The purpose of the report is to look into the increasing use of biotechnology for purposes that go beyond therapy, go beyond the domains of medicine and healing. Biotechnology is being used to build both weapons (e.g., engineered epidemics) and toys (glow-in-the-dark fish). It is altering human bodies and minds to build better muscles for athletes and to select genes for intelligence in children. It is also searching for the fountain of youth. Humans have always dreamed about and prayed for immortality. Wouldn't we all want to be the mad scientist who creates the elixir that will keep us young forever? A number of scientists are actively pursuing research that would extend the human life span, perhaps indefinitely. With the astonishing pace of biotechnological research, the dream of immortality seems just a shade closer to reality.

But what is the human natural life span? 80? 90? 120? Scientists do not seem to agree. Some argue that humans have reached the peak of their potential for life expectancy. As we age, parts begin to give out. We are simply not designed to last. There are biological limits—cell death, cessation of cell regeneration—that place an outer limit of about 80 to 90 years for most people. The few who live beyond this mark are anomalies. Other scientists argue that although there are important biological limits to how much the life span can increase, we have not yet reached our potential, which may lie somewhere around 120 to 130 years.

But some people are not content with 130 years. They want more. They want immortality, which they see as technologically feasible—there are no biological reasons, they argue, why death cannot be put off indefinitely. Death is a problem just waiting for a solution. As evidence, they note that the human life span has gradually been increasing, from about 47 in 1900 to about 77 now (in Western industrialized countries—lifespan in some third-world countries is still about 47). There is no reason, they argue, not to see the life span increase by several years each decade, indefinitely.

Perhaps the most well-studied and effective age-extension method is the calorie-restricted diet. Since the 1930s, research on animals has consistently shown that a severe restriction, of at least 60 percent of normal, will add years of life and retard the decline of physical and neurological functions. Although the mechanisms are not yet well-understood, the life-extension possibilities are incontrovertible.

Scientists are now looking at the possibilities of gene alternation to extend life. Studies of nematodes suggest that altering certain genes can extend the life of the worms. These techniques may also have application in humans, though as the President's Council on Bioethics points out, mutating genes can have serious effects on the organism. Biologists have also recently discovered a class of chemicals that might mimic the effects of the calorie-restricted diet. Resveratol, found in red wines, is of particular interest.

Not surprisingly, age-extension research has attracted attention as a potential moneymaker. For example, David Sinclair, an assistant professor at Harvard who has been working on Resveratol, hopes to start a company soon that will sell anti-aging pills. Sinclair is just one of many scientists and entrepreneurs trying to break into the age-extension market (with company names like Elixir Pharmaceuticals, LifeGen Technologies, Longenity, Rejuvenon).

One of the central questions is, What human goals and interests does biotechnology serve? Are there some priority issues, like alleviating suffering, that should be the focus of research? If biotechnology is aimed at improving human lives, how does age-extension research fit? Is death to be viewed as a problem that must be overcome, or at least averted? Is age-extension research frivolous, the pet problem of a few death-obsessed scientists? Or of money-obsessed scientists?

As the President's Council on Bioethics notes, it may not be age itself that bothers us—indeed, as we age we become rich with experience and wisdom. It is the aging process that is a drag: the deteriorating of our bodies, the arthritis, the thin skin, the poor vision and hearing, the stooped back, the addled mind. Age-extension research is essentially research into how to avert, retard, and alter the aging process itself, how to stave off the decline, and how to extend the active, healthy years.

Discussion Questions

1. Are there any moral reasons to be concerned about age-extension research?

2. What might be some of the social consequences of extending the human life span by 30 or 40 years?

3. Is death a disease?

4. Since overpopulation is already a serious global issue, isn't age extension an ethically problematic research agenda?

Resources

HALL, STEPHEN S. 2003. *Merchants of Immortality: Chasing the Dream of Human Life Extension.* Boston: Houghton Mifflin.

International Longevity Center Web site. www.ilcusa.org.

KOLATA, GINA. 2003. "Could We Live Forever?" *New York Times,* November 11, D6.

Max Planck Institute for Demographic Research. 2003. "Causes and Consequences of Increasing Longevity." www.demogr.mpg.de/general/ structure/division1/lab-sl/61.htm (accessed November 15, 2003).

National Institute on Aging Web site. www.nia.nih.gov/about/faq.htm (accessed November 15, 2003).

OLSHANSKY, JAY, and BRUCE CARNES Web site. www. thequestforimmortality. com.

OLSHANSKY, S. JAY, BRUCE A. CARNES, and ROBERT N. BUTLER. 2003. "If Humans Were Built to Last." *Scientific American* 13, no. 2 (August): 94–100.

POLLACK, ANDREW. 2003. "Forget Botox. Anti-Aging Pills May Be Next." *New York Times,* September 21, sec. 3, p. 1.

The President's Council on Bioethics. 2003. "Beyond Therapy: Biotechnology and the Pursuit of Happiness." www.bioethics.gov/reports/ beyondtherapy (accessed October 22, 2003).

THE SCHIAVOS

Terri Schiavo has been in a coma for 13 years. While she has lain quietly in a hospice bed, a bitter fight has been raging around her—all of it centered on whether she should live. Terri's own battle began when she was just 26. No one is completely sure what happened, but the best guess is that she suffered a heart attack from an acute potassium deficiency, probably caused by bulimia. Because her heart had stopped beating several minutes before the paramedics arrived, she suffered severe brain damage. She is now in what doctors call a persistent vegetative state (PVS). Patients in PVS "show no evidence of awareness of self or environment; no evidence of sustained, reproducible behavior, purposeful behavioral response to stimuli; no evidence of language comprehension or expression." Still, they have sufficiently preserved hypothalamic and brain stem autonomic function to permit survival with medical and nursing care (Goetz 2003). Patients who have been in PVS for more than three months after anoxic injury are not expected to recover.

Terri Schiavo is on life support, which means that although she breathes on her own, she is unable to swallow and would be unable to survive without intravenous feeding and hydration. Withholding food or water from a patient is repugnant to some people, but most health professionals consider this a humane and appropriate course of medical treatment.

Terri's husband, Michael, has been fighting for about six years to have her feeding tube removed. He believes that there is no hope of recovery for Terri and that it is in her best interest to be allowed to die. This is, he thinks, what she would have wanted. Michael has tried three times in court to win the right to allow Terri to die. Twice he has won his case only to have it overturned a few days later. For now, the feeding tube is in and Terri remains alive in a persistent vegetative state. But with medical and legal opinion on the side of allowing her to die, it is likely that the tube will once again be removed—perhaps for the final time.

Terri's parents, Mary and Robert Schindler, think that Terri should be fed indefinitely. In their view, she is very much alive, and removing her feeding tubes would be murder. They also hold out hope a miracle will bring Terri back to consciousness. Part of what drives the Schindlers' fight is that they believe Terri is "in there" somewhere. They think she responds to them when they visit her at the hospice. Her eyes are open, she makes movements, occasionally she smiles. Doctors say that these movements are involuntary and that her apparent responses to human interaction are random.

Other people with no direct relation to Terri's case have joined the battle, mostly on the side of Terri's parents. The Christian right has made Terri's case a publicity cause in their battle to defend "life." This is a deliberate move to expand the sphere of "pro-life" beyond abortion to include all assaults against the sacredness of life: physician-assisted suicide, removal of life support, or any other actions that might "artificially" shorten one's life (with the exception of capital punishment). Terri's parents have willingly joined with the Right in making Terri's cause public. The Web site "terrisfight.org" contains photos and even downloadable videos of Terri seeming to respond to her parents and to other stimuli.

Jeb Bush, the governor of Florida, has gained political points with the Right in his move to prevent Terri's death. The so-called Terri's Bill, passed six days after Michael won court approval to remove Terri's feeding tube, was a last-ditch effort to prevent Terri's death. The bill allowed Jeb Bush to issue an executive order to restart artificial nutrition and hydration for Terri. So, after six days, the feeding tube was reinserted, and the battle continued. President George Bush lent his support a week later, saying of his brother's actions, "He did the right thing."

The Florida courts appointed an independent guardian for Terri, to make medical decisions in her "best interests." According to the guardian, there is "no reasonable medical hope" that Terri's condition will improve. The guardian believes that the feeding tube should be removed.

No one is sure what Terri would have wanted. The night she plunged into coma, she was young and healthy and probably had no reason to think she would fall terribly ill. She left no advance directive, no written record of what her end-of-life wishes might be, how she might view being in a persistent vegetative state, what kind of life she would consider worth living.

Discussion Questions

1. Is there a right to die?

2. Who should make end-of-life decisions? Should Terri's husband, her parents, her guardian, the Florida legislature, or someone else have the final say in whether Terri should be kept alive?

3. Is it ever ethical to remove someone's feeding tube, when this is the only thing keeping the person alive? Does removing the tube allow nature to take its course, or is it the equivalent of murder?

4. What is the connection, if any, between the issue of life support and the issue of abortion?

Resources

CALLAHAN, DANIEL. 1983. "On Feeding the Dying." *Hastings Center Report* 13 (October): 22.

GOETZ, CHRISTOPHER G. 2003. "Persistent Vegetative State." In *Textbook of Clinical Neurology*, 2nd ed. Elsevier. http://home.mdconsult.com/das/book/body/230706541/1158/11.html (accessed December 7, 2003).

GOODNOUGH, ABBY. 2003. "With His Wife in Limbo, Husband Can't Move On." *New York Times*, November 2, A14.

GRUBB, A. 1995. "Withdrawal of Artificial Hydration and Nutrition: Incompetent Adult." *Medical Law Review* 3, no. 3 (Autumn): 311–16.

LYNN, JOANNE, and JAMES CHILDRESS. 1983. "Must Patients Always Be Given Food and Water?" *Hastings Center Report* 13 (October): 18.

Habitat and *Humanity*

Troublesome Trinkets

Famine in Ethiopia

'A Hunting We Will Go . . .

Glofish

Ecoterrorism: Kill the Hummers!

War Is Terrorism

Dolphin Parks

Eating Sea Turtles

PBDE and the Precautionary Principle

Canned Hunts

Cosmetic Surgery for Pets

O Canada, How Could You?

〰️ TROUBLESOME TRINKETS

The shelves of America's stores are crammed with colorful trinkets and baubles: glass bead necklaces, cheap opal bracelets, silver earrings. For a few dollars, we can follow the impulse to have something brightly colored. Our children can pass out trinkets as birthday party favors, to be worn once and then tossed into the garbage. Yet each of these inexpensive trinkets has a history that the buyer rarely understands.

One example of the troublesome trinkets cause was reported in the *New York Times* on June 18, 2003. We read the story of Hu Zhiguo, a 44-year-old who worked in a factory called Lucky Gems and Jewels that makes cheap necklaces from iridescent stones. Mr. Hu is suffering from a disease that Chinese workers call "dust lung"—what doctors call silicosis. Silicosis and other severe respiratory diseases are common, even epidemic, among factory workers like Mr. Hu. So, too, are circulatory and neurological problems related to the inhalation of silicon dioxide, which is trapped in the quartz, minerals, rocks, and sand that get blasted and ground into jewelry and figurines. The factory where stones such as opal are cut into jewelry-sized pieces is heavy with this dust—it hangs in the air like fog and turns the blue factory-issue uniforms a chalky white. A safety inspection of Lucky by the Huizhou Center for Disease Control reported silica levels in the Lucky factory 70 times higher than Chinese safety codes allowed. Mr. Hu's case was not unique: Many workers in the Lucky factory became ill with silicosis.

The Lucky factory represents one small piece of a much larger problem for poor Chinese laborers. The International Labor Organization estimates that China had almost 400,000 deaths from occupational illness in 2002, a figure that probably greatly underrepresents the actual number. Tens of millions of migrant workers like Mr. Hu—men and women who have moved from rural China to the industrial centers like Shuang Tu—work for less than a dollar an hour, with no health insurance or employment contract. Lucky exports most of its cheap jewelry to the United States, which has a thriving market for the trinkets. China is currently Asia's top exporter to the United States.

According to the U.S. General Accounting Office, a sweatshop is "an employer that violates more than one federal or state labor, industrial homework, occupational safety and health, workers' compensation, or industry registration law." Sweatshop Watch defines a sweatshop as a workplace in which workers are subject to "extreme exploitation, including the absence of a living wage or benefits; poor working conditions, such as health and safety hazards; and arbitrary discipline" (www.sweatshopwatch.org/swatch/industry/).

Mr. Hu is now too sick even to lift a bag of rice. He has returned to his rural hometown, where he is unable even to help his wife run a small fruit stand. His 16-year-old son will have to drop out of school to support the family, since Mr. Hu cannot work and will likely die soon.

Jewelry is only one small segment of the much larger apparel industry, and the working conditions in jewelry factories represent the tip of a much larger iceberg. Apparel is the most global of all manufacturing sectors and employs the largest workforce of any manufacturing industry. According to Behind the Label, approximately 80 percent of apparel workers producing goods for U.S. markets work under sweatshop conditions (www.behindthelabel.org/pdf/Retailindus.pdf). Some of the popular brands targeted by human rights and fair labor organizations include

> GAP, Inc. (one of eight defendants in a lawsuit over sweatshop conditions in Saipan)
> Levi Strauss (another of the defendants)
> Wal-Mart Stores
> Guess?
> Lord & Taylor
> Nike

Discussion Questions

1. Do American consumers have a responsibility to foreign workers who produce the goods they buy?

2. Should consumers refuse to buy products made by Lucky Gems and Jewels?

3. Is shopping a *morally* significant activity?

4 Assess the argument "A sweatshop job is better than no job."

Resources

Behind the Label. 2003. "Retailers: Responsible for the Global Sweatshop Crisis." www.behindthelabel.org/pdf/Retailindus.pdf (accessed November 5, 2003).

Co-op America's Guide to Ending Sweatshops. www.sweatshops.org (accessed November 5, 2003).

Human Rights Watch. www.hrw.org (accessed November 5, 2003).

KAHN, JOSEPH. 2003. "Making Trinkets in China, and a Deadly Dust." *New York Times,* June 18, A1.

Sweatshop Watch. www.sweatshopwatch.org (accessed November 5, 2003).

FAMINE IN ETHIOPIA

For many people around the world, the problem of famine is indelibly linked with images of children starving to death during Ethiopia's devastating drought of 1984–85. With their swollen bellies and glazed, beseeching eyes, Ethiopia's children gazed up at us from UNICEF stamps and Save the Children posters. American mothers admonished their children: "Eat your peas; there are children starving to death in Africa who would be grateful for a handful of peas!"

Jump to 2002. Ethiopia is again plunging into a potentially catastrophic famine. According to the World Food Program (WFP), the failure of both the belg (short) and the meher (long) rains will again cause a major drought. Somewhere between 11.3 and 14.3 million people—20 percent of Ethiopia's population—will need food aid in order to avert hunger and starvation. The amount of aid needed to prevent a humanitarian disaster is estimated by the WFP to be equivalent to about $500 million in U.S. dollars. Without aggressive and immediate international response, this famine will likely be far more devastating than the 1984–85 famine that killed more than 1 million Ethiopians.

The explanations for Ethiopia's recurring crises are complex and controversial. Geographic bad luck is certainly one part of the equation. Eastern Africa is susceptible to drought, and because Ethiopia relies mainly on rain-fed agriculture, less than normal rainfall can be devastating. Yet many countries (Egypt, for example) rely on rain-fed agriculture and are still able to withstand the vagaries of nature. Drought should be understood, then, as only a proximal cause of famine.

The population of Ethiopia is extremely vulnerable to natural disaster because of a basic lack of infrastructure, development, and public health programs. The country is one of the poorest in the world. It ranks 168 on the United Nations Human Development Index, very close to the bottom. Life expectancy at birth is only 43.9 years. Over three-quarters of the population live in poverty. Adult illiteracy is over 60 percent. More than three-quarters of the population drink untreated water—with major implications for public health. More than half the country's people are sick with HIV/AIDS. Ethiopia has for more than a decade been in and out of war with neighboring Eritria, draining money from human development projects into arms and ammunition.

How much should governments around the world give to help relieve this crisis? Relief agencies have urged Western governments not only to provide direct aid (money for food and non-food assistance) but also to put pressure on local governments in Africa to address long-term issues of development and infrastructure. The U.S. Congress approved $100 million in food and non-food aid to Ethiopia; relief agencies in the United States have asked Congress for $350 million more. The United States has used the humanitarian argument to support the invasion of Iraq, among other reasons. If we are concerned about human suffering, shouldn't we be more active in places like Ethiopia? James Morris, of the World Food Program, asks, "How is it that we routinely accept a level of suffering and hopelessness in Africa that we would never accept in any other part of the world?" (Kristof 2003). (Although $450 million is a large sum, note, for comparison, that in 2003 the U.S. Congress approved $20 billion for reconstruction in Iraq; 20 billion is about 40 times more than 450 million.)

What about the individual? What can and should we do, individually, to help? Do we have any moral obligation to respond to the crisis in Ethiopia? Many people are bothered by the thought of famine on the other side of the world and they do various things to help. Some give money to a relief organization such as Food for the Hungry, Bread for the World, Catholic Relief Services, Lutheran World Relief, Africare, Mennonite Central Committee, or Oxfam America. Others give money to their church, since many of the relief projects are church-based. Still others sponsor a child through an organization such as Children International, Save the Children, or Compassion International, giving perhaps $10 or $20 a month to help a particular child in need. And still others pray for those in Ethiopia. But how much is enough?

Philosopher Peter Singer argued in a famous 1972 essay that if it is in our power to prevent something bad from happening (such as people starving to death), without "sacrificing anything of comparable moral importance," we have a moral responsibility to do it. Proximity has no relevance in our responsibilities to others: We thus have a responsibility to help those suffering from famine as much as we can without seriously compromising our livelihood. Singer proposes that we give on the order of about 30 percent of our income to help those in need. Is this asking too much?

Discussion Questions

1. Do we have a moral responsibility to give aid to avert starvation in Ethiopia?

2. What kind of aid should we give: money, time and effort, political actions (e.g., writing to our government to urge sending of aid)?

3. How much should we give?

4. Is it our government's responsibility? Or does responsibility lie with each individual?

5. Do the causes of famine make any difference in whether and how we should respond?

Resources

AIKEN, WILLIAM, and HUGH LA FOLLETTE. 1995. *World Hunger and Morality*. 2nd ed. Englewood Cliffs, NJ: Prentice Hall.

BEARAK, BARRY. 2003. "Why People Still Starve." *New York Times Magazine*, July 13, 32ff.

Disaster News Network. 2003. "Ethiopia Famine Looms." www.disasternews.net/news/news.php?articled+1808 (accessed November 5, 2003).

Food for the Hungry. 2003. "History of Famine." www.ethiopiafamine.com/ (accessed November 5, 2003).

KRISTOF, NICHOLAS D. 2003. "Ethiopia's Dying Children." *New York Times*, May 13, A31.

MATHEWS, JODI. 2003. "Famine in Ethiopia Could Rival 1984–85." www.ethicsdaily.com (accessed November 5, 2003).

Relief Web. 2003. "Ethiopia." www.reliefweb.int/w/rwb.nsf/ByCountry/Ethiopia (accessed November 5, 2003).

SINGER, PETER. 1972. "Famine, Affluence, and Morality." *Philosophy and Public Affairs* 1: 229–43.

United Methodist Committee on Relief, General Board of Global Ministries. 2003. "Ethiopia Famine: UMCOR's Response." http://gbgm-umc.org/uncor/emergency/ethiopia.cfm (accessed November 5, 2003).

World Food Program. 2003. "World Hunger—Ethiopia." www.wfp.org/
country_brief/intexcountry.asp?country=231 (accessed November 10,
2003).

'A HUNTING WE WILL GO . . .

Girl Scout Troop 34 of Fairbanks, Alaska, took part in an unusual
service project. On invitation from the Alaska Department of Fish
and Game, the girls (ages 10 to 12), participated in a flood-
management program. With their families, the girls learned to
locate beaver dens, how to trap the animals, and how to kill and
skin them. The troop caught two beavers and planned to make
mittens and hats made out of the tanned pelts. Some animal-rights
groups were upset. A spokeswoman for People for the Ethical
Treatment of Animals said, "We think it sends a very bad message
that when animals cause a problem you kill them." Girl Scouts
should encourage girls to be "stewards of wildlife, not abusers."

Consider this issue: beavers are notorious for causing problems with waterways; they build dams and disrupt water flow. Yet
there are ways to address flooding issues while leaving beavers
intact. Indeed, beavers are critical to maintaining wetlands; they
are on the list of America's "keystone" species—meaning that they
are a crucial link in the survival of many other plants and animals.
Since wetlands are particularly threatened, it may be important to
address flooding issues without disrupting whole ecosystems. It is
often possible to resolve beaver problems by using flow devices
that move water underneath or through beaver dams so that
beavers get to build yet water continues to flow.

Discussion Questions

1. Is Troop 34 "sending a bad message"?

2. If the girls had been learning to hunt for food, would the
   ethics of the case have changed?

3. Can one be a "steward of wildlife" and still kill animals?

Resources

Associated Press. 2003. "No Knitting in This Troop." *Longmont Daily Times-Call*, November 12, A3.

GLOFISH

There have long been glow-in-the-dark toys—constellations, superballs, plastic snakes—but now you can have a real live glow-in-the-dark fish. The bright red fish lives and breathes—and it turns fluorescent under ultraviolet light. To make the GloFish, as it is called, a zebra fish (normally silver and black) was genetically enhanced with a gene from sea coral.

The GloFish is not the first living creature to be made to glow in the dark. In 2000, French researchers announced the creation of Alba, a rabbit whose eyes, whiskers, and fur glow green under a black light. Alba was created by splicing jellyfish genes into the rabbit's genes. Alba was meant to serve as the centerpiece for a work by the artist Eduardo Kac and was designed (according to Kac) to draw attention to the questions raised by genetic manipulation of living beings. Before this, in 1997, Japanese researchers spliced jellyfish genes into mice. This project was designed to provide a new kind of animal model for studying biological processes: The luminescent genes can be used to tag proteins, which would allow scientists to track the effect of certain drugs on the human body.

The GloFish has given opponents of genetic engineering a new target. The Center for Food Safety, a Washington, D.C.–based group, is trying to halt the sale of GloFish until a careful review of the ecological effect of the fish has been carried out. Otherwise, we may be creating an unintended environmental disaster: the fish may inadvertently wind up in waterways and wreak havoc on natural ecosystems.

The GloFish is not being used for medical or other scientific research; instead, it is being sold as a novelty pet. A gimmick.

And this is the basis of some of the most heated criticism of the GloFish: there is nothing humanly significant about their creation. Humans have manipulated and degraded another life form simply for amusement—and this is immoral. It shows a callous disregard for the value of life.

Yorktown Technologies, which is selling the GloFish, is conscious of the ethical implications of its product and has, on its GloFish Web site, a page titled "GloFish™ Guiding Ethical Principles."

- *Environmental safety first.* The company claims to do careful testing on all new lines of fluorescent fish, making sure that growth rates, temperature sensitivities, and mating success are equivalent to nonfluorescent fish of the same species.

- *Humane treatment of fish.* The company claims that its breeding and handling practices are humane, and it encourages its customers "to remember that, while unique, beautiful, and interesting, these fish are living creatures, not toys, and should be treated with the utmost care."

- *Advancement of scientific research.* The company takes pride in the fact that the GloFish was developed for use in environmental monitoring. Researchers at the National University of Singapore were working on "bio-sentinels"— biological organisms that can signal the presence of certain pollutants in an ecosystem. The GloFish was a by-product of an effort to help remediate environmental pollution.

Discussion Questions

1. Do fish have rights? Do any animals have rights?

2. Is genetically altering an animal wrong?

3. Assess the "playing God" argument.

4. Does the fact that GloFish were designed for amusement, not for some higher purpose, make a moral difference? What would constitute higher purposes?

Resources

Associated Press. 2003. "First Genetically Altered Pet Faces California Challenge." *Daily Times-Call,* December 3, A7.

GloFish Web site. www.glofish.com.

GORMAN, JAMES. 2003. "When Fish Fluoresce, Can Teenagers Be Far Behind?" *New York Times,* December 2, D3.

POLLACK, ANDREW. 2003. "Gene-Altering Revolution Is About to Reach the Local Pet Store: Glow-in-the-Dark Fish." *New York Times,* November 22, A11.

ECOTERRORISM: KILL THE HUMMERS!

In August 2003, a fire swept through a warehouse at a southern California auto dealership, destroying 20 sport utility vehicles, most of them Hummer H2s. That same night, cars at several other dealerships in West Covina, California, were spray-painted with slogans like "Fat, Lazy Americans." A group called the Earth Liberation Front (ELF)—perhaps the best-known group of "ecoterrorists" in the United States—claimed responsibility.

Sometimes the term "ecological terrorism" or "environmental terrorism" is applied to cases in which a state, group, or individual destroys or threatens to destroy the environment as an act of violence or war. For example, the burning of Kuwait's oil wells during the Persian Gulf War was an act of environmental terrorism, with profoundly damaging effects for people in Kuwait and all over the world. The defoliation of South Vietnam with Agent

Orange, although it may have had tactical significance in terms of rooting out the enemy, was also clearly an act of environmental terrorism.

More often, though, the term is used to describe people who seek to protect nature from those who harm it. "Ecoterrorism" in this sense covers a wide range of criminal activities intended not only to prevent environmental damage but also to make strong political statements about saving nature. Perhaps the most familiar form of ecoterrorism is known as tree spiking. This takes the more peaceful logging protests—people sitting in trees or chaining themselves to trunks to stop the saw—a step further. Activists infiltrate a forest and drive metal spikes into random trees in a section slated for clear-cutting. Timber companies must delay cutting until the spikes have been located, often at the cost of hundreds of thousands of dollars of lost time. Other kinds of ecoterrorism might involve sabotaging construction equipment (sugar in the gas tank of the tractor), setting fire to new developments, or smashing windows.

The Earth Liberation Front has claimed responsibility for a number of "actions." Here, for example, are a few of the many for which they have claimed responsibility since 2001:

- Spiking trees in the Otter Wing Timber Sale in the Nez Perce National Forest and, in a separate incident, in parts of the Upper Greenhorn Timber sale in the Gifford Pinchot National Forest.

- Sabotaging the biotechnology building at the University of Idaho, to protest genetic engineering.

- Burning down the offices of the Superior Lumber Company in Glendale, Oregon.

- Setting fire to a luxury home going up in a subdivision of Longmont, Colorado.

- Setting fire to parts of a Vail ski resort, causing an estimated $12 million in damage.

- Setting fire to a government truck and spray-painting "Earth Liberation Front," "Forest Rapers," and other graffiti on Forest Service buildings and trucks in Detroit, Oregon.

The ELF usually sends some kind of media message with each action. For example, the day after the fires at Vail, an e-mail was sent to the sheriff's department and local newspapers:

> ATTN: News Director, On behalf of the lynx, five buildings and four ski lifts at Vail were reduced to ashes on the night of Sunday, October 18th. The 12 miles of roads and 885 acres of clear-cuts will ruin the last, best lynx habitat in the state. Putting profits ahead of Colorado's wildlife will not be tolerated. This action is just a warning. We will be back if this greedy corporation continues to trespass into wild and unroaded areas. For your safety and convenience, we strongly advise skiers to choose other destinations until Vail cancels its inexcusable plans for expansions. Earth Liberation Front.

According to critics, the actions taken by the ELF are criminal and fit the FBI's definition of terrorism: "the unlawful use of force or violence against persons or property to intimidate or coerce a government, the civilian population, or any segment thereof, in furtherance of political or social objectives."

The ELF and its supporters believe that their acts are not "terrorism" but, rather, civil disobedience. ELF members see themselves as political activists, working to protect nature in whatever ways they can. The ELF claims that no one has ever been injured by one of their protests. Although its acts are certainly illegal (as are all acts of civil disobedience), they are never violent, in the sense of causing direct physical injury. It is obvious to them that polite policy work, which groups like the Sierra Club and the Audubon Society do so well, are ineffective and overly compromised. Craig Rosebraugh, spokesperson for the ELF, writes,

> I fully praise those individuals who take direct action, by any means necessary, to stop the destruction of the natural world and threats to all life. They are the heroes, risking their freedom and lives so that we as a species as well as all life forms can continue to exist on the planet. In a country so fixated on monetary wealth and power, these brave environmental advocates are engaging in some of the most selfless activities possible.
>
> — (Rosebraugh 2003)

Discussion Questions

1. Is the ELF engaging in nonviolent civil protest, or is the group committing crimes?

2. Are ELF's actions justified?

3. Would our ethical assessment be any different if the ELF were acting against environmentally irresponsible individuals (vandalizing random SUVs) instead of against environmentally destructive corporations (destroying Hummers on the lot)?

Resources

ABBEY, EDWARD, and DOUGLAS BRINKLEY. 2000. *The Monkey Wrench Gang*. St. Helens, OR: Perennial (republication).

ARNOLD, RON. 1997. *Ecoterror—The Violent Agenda to Save Nature*. Bellevue, WA: Free Enterprise Press.

ARNOLD, RON. 1998. *Ecology Wars: Environmentalism as if People Mattered*. Bellevue, WA: Merril Press (reissued edition).

Earth Liberation Front Web site. www.earthliberationfront.com (accessed January 16, 2004).

FOREMAN, DAVE. 1993. *Confessions of an Eco-Warrior*. New York: Three Rivers Press (reprint edition).

FOREMAN, DAVE, and BILL HAYWOOD. 1985. *Ecodefense: A Field Guide to Monkeywrenching*. Tucson, AZ: Ned Ludd Books.

GLICK, DANIEL. 2003. *Powder Burn: Arson, Money, and Mystery on Vail Mountain*. New York: PublicAffairs.

MANES, CHRISTOPHER. 1991. *Green Rage: Radical Environmentalism and the Unmaking of Civilization*. Boston: Back Bay Books (reprint edition).

ROSEBRAUGH, CRAIG. 2003. "Craig Rosebraugh on Ecoterrorism." *Green Nature*. www.greennature.com/article860.html (accessed November 15, 2003).

SCARCE, RIK, and DAVID ROSS BROWER. 1990. *Eco Warriors: Understanding the Radical Environmental Movement*. Chicago: Noble Press.

WATSON, PAUL. 1993. *Earthforce! An Earth Warrior's Guide to Strategy.* La Canada, CA: Chaco Press.

ZAKIN, SUSAN. 1995. *Coyotes and Town Dogs: Earth First! And the Radical Environmental Movement.* New York: Penguin USA.

WAR IS TERRORISM

The bumper sticker reads: WAR IS TERRORISM. Is it?

Discussion Questions

1. Is there such a thing as a just war?

2. Is there such a thing as just terrorism?

Resources

ELSHTAIN, JEAN BETHKE. 2004. *Just War Against Terror.* New York: Basic Books.

FALK, RICHARD A. 2002. *The Great Terror War.* Redford, MI: Olive Branch Press.

WALZER, MICHAEL. 2000. *Just and Unjust Wars: A Moral Argument with Historical Illustrations.* 3rd ed. New York: Basic Books.

DOLPHIN PARKS

Have you ever dreamed of swimming with dolphins? Well, now you can "experience the dream" at Dolphin Fantaseas, an American-owned dolphin park in Antigua. It is part of a rapidly growing form of entertainment: dolphin parks can be found in Florida, Mexico, the Bahamas, and elsewhere. For about $100, you can spend 30 minutes in a tank with a live dolphin, touching its skin and even holding on to its flipper while it swims. You can also buy video footage of your experience, a T-shirt, and other dolphin memorabilia. More and more tourists, bored with simply basking in the sun on the beach, are turning to dolphin parks for a rich, rewarding experience.

But not everyone is attracted to these dolphin parks, least of all (one might surmise) the dolphins themselves. Animal activists have been aggressively protesting the keeping of dolphins in captivity for many years and are distressed by the increasing popularity of dolphin parks as tourist attractions.

The world's 40 or more species of dolphins are marine mammals belonging to the order Cetacea (other cetaceans include whales and porpoises). They are considered one of nature's most intelligent creatures. They are highly social: they live and travel together in schools, communicate with one another these using a sophisticated language of whistles, screeches, and clicks, and display caregiving behaviors such as supporting a sick or injured animal at the water's surface, to prevent it from drowning.

The bottlenose (*Tursiops truncatus*) is one of the most widely used dolphins in marine parks. Although live captures of the bottlenose have depleted certain local populations around the world, the species is still generally plentiful. The accidental catch of dolphins in fishing nets—particularly purse seine nets used to catch tuna—is by far the most serious threat to the species.

Dolphin parks are legal, although the dolphins in the parks have sometimes been captured and exported in violation of the CITES rules, the Convention on International Trade in Endangered Species, under which the bottlenose dolphin is an "Appendix II" species—not currently threatened but in danger of becoming so unless trade is closely controlled. An estimated 3,000 dolphins are in captivity around the world.

One of the largest attractions for those in the dolphin park business is the income: they may make as much as $7,500 on a single dolphin in a single day. It is also a lucrative business for those who hunt and sell wild dolphins to the parks. A "green" or newly captured dolphin will bring anywhere from $40,000 to $70,000. Dolphins can sometimes also be rented out, with an option to buy. Those in the business claim that dolphin parks serve to discourage the destructive and dangerous practice of trying to swim with dolphins in the wild.

Dolphin parks and other marine parks and aquariums claim to be important educational facilities. By allowing people to see and learn about, sometimes even touch, marine life, these places build an appreciation of the life that fills the oceans. The dolphin defenders, however, see things differently: marine parks teach, through example, that it is acceptable to keep creatures like dolphins in captivity and to use them as a source of entertainment. To the argument that marine parks serve as important research facilities—where dolphins can be studied, leading to better conservation programs—dolphin defenders will note that researching captive animals is useful only for understanding captive animals and that it tells us little to nothing about preserving dolphins in their natural habitat.

One of the central arguments of dolphin defenders is that dolphins suffer from being held captive. The World Society for the Protection of Animals argues that when taken from their pods, or families, the dolphins suffer from loneliness. In nature, dolphins live in close-knit families called pods. They are also free-ranging, often covering as much as 100 miles a day in open waters. Yet, to meet legal animal welfare requirements, their pens must be only as wide and long as 24 feet, less than one-third the length of a regular lap pool. In captivity, the normal life span of a dolphin is often cut short, and the animals suffer from health problems related to stress and to living in highly chlorinated water. The dolphin, like the whale, is an acoustic animal and uses echolocation, or sonar, to communicate with other dolphins and also to hunt for fish. According to the dolphin activists, putting a dolphin in a pool with concrete walls is like sentencing a human to life in a room of mirrors—the chaotic sensory overload is a recipe for insanity.

The actual capture of the dolphins is also of concern. As activist group In Defense of Animals (2003) describes it,

> The capture of wild dolphins and whales is violent, cruel and disruptive to entire communities of cetaceans and the ecosystems in which they live. One capture method involves chasing dolphins to the point of exhaustion with high speed boats. The dolphins are then netted and dragged aboard. . . . Another

method also involves chasing the animals with boats and herding them into enclosed bays or makeshift sea pens, where they are trapped and frequently separated from family members.

Discussion Questions

1. Are dolphin parks immoral?

2. Do humans have certain moral responsibilities to dolphins? If so, what are those responsibilities?

3. Is the use of animals for human entertainment wrong?

Resources

The Alliance of Marine Mammal Parks and Aquariums. 2003. "Dolphin Family Vacation." www.ammpa.org/dolphvac.html (December 19, 2003).

CAVALIERI, PAOLA. 2001. *The Animal Question: Why Non-human Animals Deserve Human Rights.* Translated by Catherine Woollard. Oxford University Press.

Convention on International Trade in Endangered Species of Wild Fauna and Flora (CITES). www.cites.org (accessed December 20, 2003).

DeGRAZIA, DAVID. 1996. *Taking Animals Seriously: Mental Life and Moral Status.* Cambridge University Press.

The Dolphin Project. www.thedolphinproject.org (accessed December 20, 2003).

GONZALEZ, DAVID. 2003. "This Is Fun, But Did Anyone Ask the Dolphins?" *New York Times,* October 2, A4.

In Defense of Animals. 2003. "The Plight of Marine Mammals." www.idausa.org/campaigns/marine/captivity/html   (accessed December 19, 2003).

POLLAN, MICHAEL. 2002. "An Animal's Place." *New York Times Magazine,* November 10.

SCULLY, MATTHEW. 2003. *Dominion: The Power of Man, the Suffering of Animals, and the Call to Mercy.* New York: St. Martin's Press.

SINGER, PETER. 2003. "Animal Liberation at 30." *New York Review of Books,* May 15, 23–28.

EATING SEA TURTLES

Extinction: To be extinguished. To no longer exist.

Wildcoast is a small nonprofit conservation group in San Diego working to preserve the threatened coastal wildlands of the Californias. One of Wildcoast's main projects is to fight for the survival of sea turtles, which are rapidly sliding toward extinction. To this end, Wildcoast is campaigning to stop all eating of sea turtles, in both the United States and Mexico, where sea turtle has long been part of the traditional diet in rural fishing villages.

Sea turtles have been swimming the earth's oceans since the Middle Triassic period (230 million years ago, the same time as the mighty *Tyrannosaurus Rex*) and represent one of the oldest continuous vertebrate lineages. These sea-living, air-breathing reptiles are wonders of nature. The leatherback turtle, for example, can weigh more than a ton and stretch some eight and a half feet. Because it can regulate its body temperature (a highly unusual adaptation for a reptile), the leatherback can dive to depths of 3,000 feet. Scientists estimate that the leatherback will likely become extinct in the next five years. A similar fate awaits all species of sea turtle that grace the oceans: the loggerhead, the olive ridley, the Kemp's ridley, the green turtle, the hawksbill, and the flatback.

Extinction, of course, is a vital mechanism of evolution: species have been going extinct since the dawn of life of earth, and new species take their place. Yet most scientists and philosophers find an important distinction between "natural" extinction and extinction that sends chills down the spine—the kind of extinction whereby species disappear like blinks of an eye and evolution is stopped in its tracks. Over the past three decades, and as a direct result of human activities, we have begun to witness an extinction of vast proportions: scientists estimate that the number of species now going extinct is between several a day and several every few seconds. It is this "unnatural" and human-induced extinction that threatens the sea turtles. They cannot handle the human encroachment into their oceans, their beaches, and their nests.

One of the major problems for the turtles is the disruption of their nesting grounds by tourists, which can cause female turtles to scuttle their egg-laying altogether or settle for a beach less suitable for survival of the hatchlings. Artificial lighting near or on beaches has a disorienting effect on baby sea turtles, who find their way to the ocean by moonlight reflected off the water. Turtles lose nesting ground when human construction and interference cause beaches to erode, yet they are also harmed when sea walls or jetties are built to prevent erosion.

Sea turtles also suffer significant harm from commercial fishing, particularly shrimp trawlers, which trap and drown them. Garbage floating in the ocean is a hazard because it often looks like food (floating plastic bags resemble jellyfish) but can choke and suffocate a turtle.

By far the most significant threat is turtle soup and turtle fillet. Green turtles are the most popular food, but all turtle species are eaten. According to Wildcoast, more than 35,000 endangered sea turtles are killed and eaten each year. Easter is an especially dangerous time for them, because they are traditionally eaten during Lent, having long been considered fish rather than meat (since they swim), although the official word from the Vatican is that sea turtle flesh is meat and should not be eaten during Lent.

Legal protection has done little to stem the slaughter. In 1990 the president of Mexico declared a permanent moratorium on capturing sea turtles, with a possible sentence of three years in jail. In the United States, they are protected under the Endangered Species Act: anyone caught harassing or harming a sea turtle can be fined up to $50,000. Despite these protections, numbers continue to plummet. According to Wildcoast, the black market trade in meat and eggs is the principal cause of this continued decline. Turtles are caught in Mexico, exported (illegally), and sold to restaurants in the United States.

Turtle activists oppose all eating of turtle meat and have been aggressive about their campaign in California. They give bad

press to restaurants that serve turtle and have a series of bill-
boards along the southern California freeways that address the
message of turtle conservation. (On one billboard, for example, is
a picture of a giant panda, with the words "You wouldn't eat this,
would you?") However, they are more cautious about their campaign when they travel into Mexico, where the eating of turtle is
part of rural fishing life. Many families have subsisted on turtle
meat for generations. Still, many of these villagers have themselves joined the fight to save the sea turtles.

Discussion Questions

1. Does it matter if the leatherback or the hawksbill goes
   extinct? Why or why not?

2. If extinction is a "natural" phenomenon, why should groups
   like Wildcoast care about the extinction of sea turtles?

3. Should people for whom turtle is a traditional source of food
   be criticized for eating it?

4. Is there a moral difference between a family from a small
   Mexican fishing village eating turtle meat as part of a
   traditional Easter meal and a couple from San Diego eating
   turtle soup in an expensive restaurant?

5. Is it legitimate for a U.S. conservation group to try to
   convince villagers in Mexico not to eat turtle, or should they
   mind their own business?

Resources

CARR, ARCHIE. 1976. *So Excellent a Fishe: A Natural History of Sea Turtles.* New York: American Museum of Natural History.

DAVIDSON, OSHA GRAY. 2003. *Fire in the Turtle House: The Green Sea Turtle and the Fate of the Ocean.* New York: PublicAffairs.

ELLIS, RICHARD. 2003. *The Empty Ocean: Plundering the World's Marine Life.* Washington, DC: Island Press.

Grupo Tortuguero de las Californias (Sea Turtle Conservation Network of the Americas). http://baja.seaturtle.org/ (accessed November 15, 2003).

Marine Turtle Newsletter. www.seaturtle.org/mtn/ (accessed December 21, 2003).

QUAMMEN, DAVID. 1997. *The Song of the Dodo: Island Biogeography in an Age of Extinctions.* New York: Scribner and Sons.

Wildcoast. www.wildcoast.net (accessed November 15, 2003).

WILSON, EDWARD O. 2003. *The Future of Life.* New York: Vintage.

PBDE AND THE PRECAUTIONARY PRINCIPLE

Could your sofa be poisoning you? Could your computer be harming children? These are the questions scientists and environmentalists are beginning to ask about a group of chemicals called polybrominated diphenyl ethers, or PBDEs. PBDEs are widely used as flame retardants: The bromine in PBDEs is highly reactive and squelches flames by grabbing up electrons. PBDEs can be found in the foam padding of furniture and car seats; in the plastics in computers, televisions, and home appliances; in the fabric in drapes, carpets, and even children's pajamas. In hard plastics and foam padding, PBDEs can make up as much as 30 percent of the material by weight. About 135 million pounds of PBDEs are manufactured worldwide each year, about half of this for use in the United States. Scientists are particularly concerned about penta-BDE (having five bromines attached to the carbon rings), which appears to be one of the most toxic of the PBDE compounds.

Though useful, PBDEs may also turn out to be extremely dangerous. Scientists are alarmed at how quickly PDBEs are building up in the environment and in human bodies. Samples of human breast milk show PBDE levels doubling about every two and a half years. High levels have also been found in human blood, wildlife, food, rural air, and in the sewage sludge being spread in huge quantities as fertilizer for food crops in the United States.

PBDEs belong to a family of chemical compounds collectively referred to as *persistent organic pollutants,* or POPs. POPs include manufactured chemicals such as PBDEs and polychlorinated biphenyls (PCBs), industrial by-products like dioxin, and a variety of pesticides, including DDT, aldrin, chlordane, dieldrin, and heptachlor. POPs share certain chemical properties: they are fat-soluble, so they accumulate in the fatty tissue of humans and others animals who ingest them, and they are chemically stable, so they can persist in the environment for long periods of time.

PBDEs have been found in every blood sample tested in the United States; they have also been found in ocean sediments, whales and dolphins, cow's milk, and salmon. These ubiquitous chemicals seem to be found just about everywhere that researchers look. Scientists are not sure exactly how PBDEs make their way from various household products into our bodies. PBDEs may enter the environment during the manufacture and disposal of materials containing the flame retardants. Some scientists believe that when foam and materials degrade, they form dust, which contains PBDEs. Others believe that eating contaminated fish or meat is the primary route of exposure for humans.

The health effects of PBDEs are poorly understood but of serious concern to some researchers. Animal studies show pronounced behavioral and memory problems in mice exposed in utero to PBDEs. Those worried about PBDEs believe that the chemicals may interfere with the functioning of thyroid hormones, which regulate the growth of a baby's neurological system. PBDEs are structurally similar to thyroid hormones—each consists of two six-carbon rings with halogens attached. In the thyroid hormone, the halogen is iodine; in PBDEs it is bromine. Researchers argue that the immediate effects on babies exposed to tainted breast milk may be losses in intelligence, memory, and hearing. PBDEs may also cause cancer and liver damage.

Environmentalists and scientists in the United States who have called for a ban on the chemicals argue that the current U.S. approach to risk assessment and scientific uncertainty—"innocent until proven guilty"—is inadequate. Unless a chemical is known to cause serious risk, its manufacture and use are acceptable. The problems with this approach are several. First, the EPA has tested only a fraction of the chemicals on the market—testing is difficult and expensive and takes time. At least a thousand new chemical compounds enter the market, and the environment, each year without any testing for safety. Testing begins, typically, once a chemical becomes suspicious—once it has caused enough harm to get people's attention. But since the effects of chemicals on organisms are often delayed (you may not develop cancer until 10 or 20 years after exposure), this approach ensures problems. Peter Montague, editor of *Rachel's Environment and Health News,* says, "Risk assessments are always 'behind the curve' and therefore always give false assurances of safety" (Montague, *Rachel's Weekly* #736).

An alternative approach to risk assessment—the approach that led to a ban on PBDEs by the European Union—is known as the *precautionary principle.* It says that decision-makers have an obligation to take preventive action to avoid harm, even before scientific certainty exists. Under this paradigm, the onus of proof rests with the manufacturer and government to thoroughly test and understand a chemical before it is allowed into use. Environmentalists note that the United States and other countries are already under an obligation to abide by the precautionary principle: the Rio Declaration signed by the United States and many other nations at the 1992 United Nations Conference on Environment and Development binds signatory governments to a precautionary approach toward environmental degradation. "Where there are threats of serious or irreversible damage, lack of full scientific certainty shall not be used as a reason for postponing cost-effective measures to prevent environmental degradation." Peter Montague defends the precautionary approach on ethical grounds: "Everyone can understand the wisdom of 'Do unto others as you would have others do unto you' and 'better safe than sorry'" (Montague, *Rachel's Weekly* #657).

The companies that manufacture PBDEs are opposed to a ban. They argue that the benefits to humans are well-known and the risks uncertain. According to the industry groups, the brominated flame retardants allow people more time to escape from a fire because they slow the burn rate. Furthermore, flame retardants are required by U.S. law. Although alternatives to PBDE flame retardants do exist (e.g., compounds with a silicon or phosphorus base), polybrominated diphenyl ethers are among the most effective and cost efficient on the market.

Discussion Questions

1. Is the precautionary principle an ethically sound approach to the use and regulation of chemicals?

2. How much risk is acceptable?

3. Can you apply the principle of "do no harm" where harms are uncertain?

4. Relate the precautionary principle to the current debate about global climate change.

Resources

COLBORN, THEO, FREDERICK S. VOM SAAL, and ANA M. SOTO. 1996. *Our Stolen Future: Are We Threatening Our Fertility, Intelligence, and Survival? A Scientific Detective Story.* Miami, FL: Dutton.
CONE, MARLA. 2003. "Cause for Alarm over Chemicals." *Los Angeles Times,* April 20, A1.
CRENSEN, MATT. 2002. "Flame-Retardant Chemical Could Prove as Serious a Pollutant as PCBs or DDT." *Environmental News Network,* January 30. www.enn.com/news/wire-stories/2002/01/01302002/ap_retardant_46266.asp (accessed July 30, 2003).
MONTAGUE, PETER. 1999. "The Uses of Scientific Uncertainty." *Rachel's Environment and Health News, Rachel's Weekly #657,* June 30. www.rachel.org/bulletin (accessed December 30, 2003).

MONTAGUE, PETER. 2001. "Here We Go Again: PBDEs." *Rachel's Environment and Health News, Rachel's Weekly #736,* October 25. www.rachel.org/bulletin (accessed December 30, 2003).

Natural Resources Defense Council. 2003. "Healthy Milk, Healthy Baby: Chemical Pollution and Mother's Milk." www.nrdc.org/breastmilk/chem10.asp (accessed December 21, 2003).

RAFFENSPERGER, CAROLYN, JOEL TICKNER, and WES JACKSON, eds. 1999. *Protecting Public Health and the Environment: Implementing the Precautionary Principle.* Washington, DC: Island Press.

STEINGRABER, SANDRA. 2001. *Having Faith: An Ecologist's Journey to Motherhood.* Scranton, PA: Perseus Publishing.

CANNED HUNTS

Vice President Dick Cheney raised the ire of the Humane Society of the United States when he took a holiday hunting trip to a private "club" in Pennsylvania. Cheney reportedly shot more than 70 pheasants and a number of mallard ducks—which would have been an impressive take out in the hills of Pennsylvania. Only the birds were stocked: They were pen-raised with the sole purpose of being released in the sights of a well-paying customer. For the Humane Society, these so-called canned hunts are unethical because a large number of caged animals are released and then slaughtered. Sometimes, tame animals sold to hunting ranches by petting zoos are even used as targets.

> Unlike situations in which animals can use their natural and instinctual abilities to escape predation, a canned hunt affords animals no such opportunity. In fact, animals may be hand-reared, fed at regular times, and moved regularly among a system of corrals and paddocks. These practices lessen the natural fear and flight response elicited by human beings, and ensure the hunters an easy target. Animals may be set up for a kill as they gather at a regular feeding area or as they move toward a familiar vehicle or person. (Humane Society 2003)

Even some avid hunters consider canned hunts contrary to the ethics of their sport because the fair-chase rules of nature are manipulated: there is nothing sporting about hunting a confined animal. The well-accepted rules of fair chase also include not baiting waterfoul, not spotlighting deer, not shooting from car windows, and not shooting from helicopters.

Canned hunts are becoming increasingly popular. The Humane Society estimates that there are at least 1,000 such hunting operations in the United States. They appeal to a certain class of hunter: corporate groups who have limited time but still want to bring home a trophy; people who are not skilled enough marksmen to "bag" a five-point elk or who lack the physical stamina for a long day's hunt. In addition to promising a successful kill, these hunting clubs (often called game ranches) offer the chance to shoot exotic game: oryx, blackbuck, gemsbok, addax, eland, aoudad, ibex, even sometimes the odd rhino or zebra. You can hunt wolf in British Columbia, cougar in Wyoming. Associated Hunting Consultants advertises an exotic hunt on a ranch near Laredo, Texas. For $3,000, a hunter can bring home an oryx, a blackbuck, a mouflon sheep, and a feral hog. Their brochure boasts, "Hunter success should be 100% on the oryx, mouflon and blackbuck."

Supporters of canned-hunt operations argue that the animals are bred in large enough numbers that even hunting exotic game does no damage. Animals bought from zoos would not survive in the wild anyway, so bringing them onto a game ranch does not alter their fate in any appreciable way. "Shooting over bait" (killing an animal when it comes to a designated feeding site) ensures a clean kill and is ultimately more humane for the animal than a botched shot in the wild. Supporters also argue on economic grounds: In Texas alone, the hunt industry brings in $1 billion a year.

Nine states have banned canned hunts, and legislation is being introduced in several other states.

Discussion Questions

1. What are the ethics of hunting?

2. Do canned hunts violate them?

3. Assess the "clean kill" argument.

4. Is hunting for sport immoral?

Resources

Humane Society of the United States. 2003. "Canned Hunts." www. hsus. org/ace/12017 (accessed December 23, 2003).

KLUGER, JEFFREY. 2002. "Hunting Made Easy." *CNN.com*. www. cnn.com/ ALLPOLITICS/time/2002/03/11/hunting.html (accessed December 23, 2003).

PACELLE, WAYNE. 2003. "Stacking the Hunt." *New York Times*, December 9, A29.

POSEWITZ, JIM. 1994. *Beyond Fair Chase: The Ethic and Tradition*. Kingwood, TX: Falcon Publishing.

Safari Club International. www.scifirstforhunters.org/content/website/ ?g11n.enc=ISO-8859-1 (accessed December 31, 2003).

SHEEHAN, LARRY et al. 1992. *The Sporting Life: A Passion for Hunting and Fishing*. New York: Clarkson Potter.

SWAN, JAMES A. 1994. *In Defense of Hunting*. New York: HarperCollins.

COSMETIC SURGERY FOR PETS

It all began when Danny's victory at the famed Crufts dog show in England was challenged. The fluffy Pekingese, named Supreme Champion, was accused of having had plastic surgery on his face. Surgical procedures to amend a dog's appearance are strictly against the rules. And although the accusations against Danny's owner were never proven, the issue of cosmetic surgery on pets came into the spotlight. Although no dog has ever been disqualified for having been surgically altered, suspicion has it that such alterations do occur. Elizabeth Tilley, an American

Pekingese breeder, was quoted in the *New York Times:* "People open nostrils, they straighten tails, they enhance the color on the ear fringing, or if a dog doesn't have a black mask, they paint one on with hair color."

Set aside for now the question of whether it is acceptable to cheat on competition rules. Is performing surgery on dogs for purely cosmetic reasons wrong, where the aim of surgery is to make a dog more competitive in a dog show? Yet what about a surgical procedure where the line between medically necessary and cosmetically appealing (for humans) is fuzzy? A number of procedures fall into this blurry between-the-lines place: ear cropping, dewclaw removal, declawing, and tail docking. Of these, tail docking seems to attract particular controversy.

Tail docking is usually performed on puppies between 2 and 10 days old, without anesthesia (which can be risky in such a young animal). One method, usually performed by a veterinarian, involves clamping the tail and cutting off the portion below the clamp. In another method called "banding"—often performed by breeders rather than vets—the tail is tied off with some kind of tourniquet, perhaps a rubber band. This cuts off the blood supply, and in a few days, the tied-off segment falls off.

Proponents and opponents of tail docking agree that the central motivation behind docking is to maintain physical characteristics that have been established for particular breeds. At least 50 breeds of dog have docked tails, including many gun dogs, terriers, rottweilers, Doberman pinschers, and boxers. This is the first and last point of agreement.

Opponents of tail docking argue that tradition must change to eliminate cruel practices—desire for a particular look is not a good justification for cutting off a dog's tail. Not only is the procedure painful, it also takes away from the dog one of its essential means of social interaction with other dogs: The tail is a key communication tool (wagging, bristling, straight). Proponents, many of whom are breeders, defend the practice as essential to maintain the physical standards of each breed. The procedure is humane and actually prevents harm to the dog by preventing injury to the tail. Hunting dogs, when tracking game through heavy underbrush, can tear their tails on thorns or catch them on branches. Opponents counter that most dogs, even of the hunting breeds, are kept as pets—so the injury-to-tail-from-heavy-underbrush argument is weak, at best. Furthermore, many traditional hunting breeds—the Irish setter, Labrador retriever, and beagle, among others—have always had long tails.

One of the key points of controversy is whether or not tail docking is painful for the puppies. (The debate is reminiscent of a similar argument over whether or not the human fetus experiences pain during the abortion procedure.) Opponents of tail docking argue that the nervous system of young puppies is highly developed and that they likely experience significant pain. They squeal and cry and then crawl to their mother for comfort. Proponents of docking claim that some puppies even sleep through the procedure, and they use the fact that puppies seek to nurse afterward as evidence that they are unaffected by the surgery.

Discussion Questions

1. Do humans have moral responsibilities toward dogs and other animals?

2. Is it wrong for humans to manipulate animals for such purposes as dog shows? Are there some justified and some unjustified examples of surgical manipulation?

3. Peter Singer argues that it is the capacity to feel pain and pleasure that confers moral standing on an animal. A dog likely has a more acute sense of pain and deprivation than a newborn baby, suggesting that we shouldn't do anything to a dog that we wouldn't do to an infant—such as perform unnecessary surgery. Assess this argument.

4. Does ownership impose certain responsibilities?

5. Is ownership an appropriate model for the relationship between dogs and humans?

Resources

In Defense of Animals. 2003. "Cosmetic Surgery: Facts." www.idausa.org (accessed January 16, 2004).
"San Francisco Panel Wants Ban on Cosmetic Surgery for Pets." May 22, 2000. www.CNN.com (accessed January 16, 2004).
TREBAY, GUY. 2003. "From Woof to Warp." *New York Times,* April 6, sec. 9, p. 1.

O CANADA, HOW COULD YOU?

On Friday, August 15, 2003, the *New York Times* ran a full-page advertisement on page 8. The half-page photo shows a person cloaked in black, his head and face completely obscured by a black cap, like an executioner. He is bending over the snow, with what looks like a red aluminum baseball bat silhouetted against the white. The bat is poised over the head of a baby seal, whose mouth gapes open in a cry. Nearby, part of another seal—perhaps the mother, perhaps another baby—is visible, lying in a bed of bloody snow.

Scrawled in blood over the photo are the dripping red words "O CANADA. HOW COULD YOU?"

Below the large photo is the following text: "Thanks to the Canadian government the infamous clubbing of baby seals is back with a vengeance. The Canadian government announced that over the next 3 years, they will allow close to 1,000,000 seals to be brutally clubbed or shot, even subsidizing the sealing industry with millions of dollars. Too many seals have already died. CANADA, STOP THE SLAUGHTER NOW." Next to the text is a close-up of a seal, gazing at you with its soft, pool-like black eyes. The advertisement asks readers to contact the prime minister of Canada and ask him to stop the hunt.

The message was paid for by the Humane Society of the United States and was presented on behalf of the World Community of Animal Protection (WCAP), which includes the International Wildlife Coalition, the Fund for Animals, the Animal Protection Institute, and a number of other animal welfare organizations.

One of the most frequent criticisms of animal rights and animal protection groups is that they employ advertising campaigns that appeal to pity and that exploit graphic images for the purposes of making people feel uncomfortable.

Discussion Questions

1. Are the WCAP's tactics deserving of moral criticism?

2. Should an organization use whatever visual tactics are most effective in making its point?

3. Should people be made aware of the horrors that animals endure?

4. Compare the use of graphic images by pro-animal activists with their use by pro-life activists.

Resources

All-creatures.org. 2004. "Seal Hunting: A Cruel Slaughter on Ice." www.all-creatures.org/articles/ar-sealhunting.html (accessed June 7, 2004).

Animals Voice. 2004. "Seal Song: The Canadian Seal Slaughter." www. animalsvoice.com/PAGES/features/seal.html (accessed June 7, 2004).

BECKOFF, MARC, and CARRON A. MEANEY. 1998. *Encyclopedia of Animal Rights and Animal Welfare.* Westport, CT: Greenwood.

Humane Society of the United States. www.husu.org.

REGAN, TOM. 1985. *The Case for Animal Rights.* Berkeley: University of California Press.

Liberty and Coercion

DanceSafe: Making Ecstasy Safer for Partyers

Banning Ephedra

Obesity: Personal or Political?

Worried about Harry Potter

Wal-Mart Keeps Its Shelves Clean

Edward "NJ Weedman" Forchion: Ganja Brings Him Closer to God

License-Plate Liberties

Pledge of Allegiance

Ed Rosenthal and Medical Marijuana

Cameras Watching Students

High School Tells Student to Remove Anti-War T-Shirt

CRACK—Get Sterilized, Get Cash

My Hummer, My Choice

"Let Those Who Ride Decide": Motorcycle Helmet Laws and Biker Rights

USA Patriot Act

≋ DANCESAFE: MAKING ECSTASY SAFER FOR PARTYERS

The drug Ecstasy, or MDMA (3,4-methylenedioxymethamphetamine), has become a wildly popular club drug. The National Institute on Drug Abuse estimated that in 1998 (the most recent year for which data were available) some 3.4 million people over the age of 12 had tried E (also called "Adam," "XTC," or "Doves") at least once.

The chemical compound in Ecstasy was originally synthesized and patented in 1941 by the German pharmaceutical company Merck. It was used in psychotherapeutic treatment until the mid-1980s, when studies on animals revealed that MDMA causes damage to nerve cells in the brain. It triggers the release of the neurotransmitter serotonin and (much like Prozac and other antidepressants) blocks the reuptake of serotonin. This explains why users say that E transports them into a state of well-being and increases their sense of empathy and compassion for others, creating a feeling of psychic and emotional openness that is rare under sober conditions.

Although research on MDMA is incomplete, studies suggest that it may permanently affect memory and thought and may damage the brain cells that release serotonin. Other long-term effects include depression, sleep disorders, paranoia, and a persistent craving for the drug. It also appears that users develop some immunity to the drug so that larger and larger doses are required to achieve the ecstatic high. In the short term, MDMA raises heart rate, blood pressure, and body temperature, often to damaging levels.

One of the most dangerous things about E is the risk of swallowing an adulterated drug containing substances more toxic than MDMA. A study published in the *Journal of the American Medical Association* in 2000 reported that about 30 percent of the "ecstasy" pills collected from rave parties around the country contained no MDMA. The most common adulterant was a drug called DMX (dextromethorphan), a cough suppressant that can cause heart problems, ataxia, and a number of other adverse health effects.

Enter DanceSafe, a nonprofit group working out of Oakland, California. The aim of the organization is what it calls "harm reduction." Assuming that kids will take drugs, what can we do to make this experience safer for them? DanceSafe volunteers show up at all-night rave parties or dance clubs and offer free testing of ecstasy pills for MDMA. Anyone at a party can bring their pill to the DanceSafe table, where a volunteer will scrape off a small bit with a razor, add a few drops of a chemical, and wait to see if it turns purple, for Ecstasy, or some other color. Then the volunteer will return the pill—MDMA, PMA, aspirin, or whatever it happens to be—and the user can decide whether or not to take it. The organization also provides educational material about the potential dangers of both MDMA and the various compounds often found in the adulterated pills.

Emanuel Sferios, the founder of DanceSafe, claims that his organization has saved lives by preventing young people from taking the more dangerous adulterated pills and by educating them about E. Because it is unreasonable to expect that young people will simply stay away from drugs, he thinks it is better to use a nonjudgmental approach: to strive for safer drug use, not no drug use.

Parents and drug enforcement officials are not so keen on the project. By offering this pill-testing service, DanceSafe implies that Ecstasy itself, when pure, is not dangerous. According to critics of DanceSafe, when you simply test a pill and hand it back to a young person, you imply that drug use is acceptable. Although its motives may be good, DanceSafe promotes drug use, and this is just plain bad.

Discussion Questions

1. Is there anything inherently wrong with drug use?

2. Is the use of substances to enter an altered state a universally desirable and common human experience, or does it somehow defile the body's natural state?

3. If MDMA were completely safe, would it be wrong to take it?

4. If legalization of the drug would lead to control of its purity, would legalization be a good idea?

5. Does DanceSafe encourage drug use? If so, is this a good argument against it?

6. How does one judge DanceSafe? Is it a simple calculation of how much good the organization appears to do (protecting people against DMX, etc.) versus how much bad (sending the message that drug use is okay)?

Resources

BAGGOTT, M., B. HEIFETS, R.T. JONES, J. MENDELSON, E. SFERIOS, and J. ZEHNDER. 2000. "Chemical Analysis of Ecstasy Pills." *Journal of the American Medical Association* 284 (17): 2190.

BECK, J., and M. ROSENBAUM. 1994. *Pursuit of Ecstasy: The MDMA Experience.* Albany: State University of New York Press.

DanceSafe Web site. www.DanceSafe.org (accessed June 20, 2003).

National Institute on Drug Abuse. 2003. "Info Facts: MDMA (Ecstasy)." www.drugabuse.gov/Infofax/ecstasy.html (accessed June 20, 2003).

BANNING EPHEDRA

The herb *ephedra sinica*, also known as ma huang or country mallow, has a long history of usefulness to humans. Ephedra stimulates the sympathetic nervous system: It causes blood vessels in the lining of the nose to constrict and dilates the bronchial tubes, making it a useful treatment for asthma and decongestion. It is also a mild stimulant: By opening up the adrenergic receptor sites found in the heart and lungs, it increases the body's basic metabolic rate and calorie consumption. It can enhance energy and alertness and is even thought to focus the mind. Ephedra has been used in Chinese medicine for more than 5,000 years.

Over the past decade or so, ephedra has also become widely available in the United States, promoted as both a weight-loss drug and an athletic-performance enhancer. The shelves of General Nutrition Center have been stocked with row after row of Metabolift, Diet Fuel, Stacker, Hydroxycut, and Ripped Fuel promising chiseled muscles and the almost-effortless melting away of body fat. Particularly in its application as a weight-loss drug, ephedra is often combined with caffeine or a natural caffeine source such as green tea, guarana, or kola nut. Although the data on ephedra are limited, studies have confirmed that it is effective as part of a weight-loss program. Particularly when combined with caffeine, it is one of the few substances proven to be helpful in weight loss. Its usefulness as a performance enhancer is less clear. The number of people using ephedra is thought to be about 12 million.

Whether or not ephedra is safe has been subject to more significant debate. While the available data suggest that it is quite safe, the Food and Drug Administration has collected a number of *Adverse Event Reports* (anecdotal reports filed by consumers or health professionals) on ephedra products. The drug came under intense scrutiny in the summer of 2002 after the sudden death of 23-year-old Orioles pitcher Steve Bechler was linked to Xenadrine RFA-1, an ephedra product. According to the FDA, ephedra poses "an unreasonable risk to the public health." The supplement has consistently been associated with relatively mild side effects like palpitations and gastrointestinal distress. There have been about 1,000 serious health events, including 100 deaths.

After Bechler's death, the commissioner of the FDA urged a ban on the use of ephedra in major-league baseball. According to the FDA, the drug is dangerous, particularly for competitive athletes whose bodies are under considerable strain from high-level training, and it is only marginally useful in improving sports performance. Ephedra is banned in the minor leagues and also in the

National Football League, Major Soccer League, and the National Collegiate Athletic Association.

In December 2003, the FDA announced a nationwide ban on the supplement, to go into effect within several months. The FDA has the authority to regulate ephedra under the Dietary Supplement Health and Education Act (DSHEA), which Congress passed in 1994. But the FDA must be able to prove that a given dietary supplement poses a significant risk of injury or illness before any restrictions may be placed on the product's use. Dietary supplement manufacturers are not required to provide any proof of safety or effectiveness prior to marketing a product— making the supplement industry essentially unregulated. (Synthetic ephedrine drug products like Sudafed and Claritin are considered drugs and, although sold over the counter, are regulated much more strictly than dietary supplements.)

Many people believe that herbs, vitamins, and other dietary supplements should be more closely scrutinized by the government. With over half the population purchasing dietary supplements each year, much more should be done to ensure their safety and efficacy. To this end, Senator Dick Durbin introduced a bill before the Senate (Senate Bill 722, Dietary Supplement Safety Act of 2003) that would give the FDA sweeping regulatory power over dietary supplements, shifting the burden of proof from the government to the supplement makers.

This move toward tighter regulation worries many people. We have a fundamental right to be in control of our own health, and this means using herbs, minerals, vitamins, or, if we want to, blue-green algae. We should have the right to pursue health as we understand it, not as the government understands it. If Durbin's bill passes, substances that have safely been used for thousands of years will be required to undergo expensive clinical testing. And when a substance becomes FDA regulated, its price invariably increases, hindering access for many consumers.

On a different tack, the supporters of ephedra argue that the obesity epidemic is a good enough reason to keep it on the shelves. Almost 40 million American adults are considered obese, almost 20 percent of the population. The yearly death toll from obesity-related health problems (diabetes, heart disease, hypertension) is about 300,000, making obesity the second most dangerous health problem (behind smoking)—far, far more dangerous, say supporters, than an herb called ephedra.

Discussion Questions

1. Should ephedra be banned by the government?

2. Do citizens have a right to pursue health in whatever ways they see fit?

3. Would the government regulation of dietary supplements unreasonably hinder this right?

4. As long as packages are clearly marked with warning labels, is there anything wrong with selling dangerous substances? (What is the difference between ephedra and tobacco?)

Resources

DREW, CHRISTOPHER. 2003. "Complaints and Support for Diet Pill at Congressional Hearing." *New York Times*, July 24, A12.

DREW, CHRISTOPHER. 2003. "Official Urges Ban of Ephedra by Baseball." *New York Times*, July 25, C19.

Ephedra Education Counsel, Consumer Information. www.ephedrafacts.com/consumer.html (accessed October 15, 2003).

Ephedra Web site. www.ephedra.net/ (accessed October 15, 2003).

Office of the Surgeon General. 2001. "Call to Action to Prevent and Decrease Overweight and Obesity." December. www.surgeongeneral.gov/topics/obesity/ (accessed October 22, 2003).

U.S. Food and Drug Administration. 2003. "Evidence on the Safety and Effectiveness of Ephedra: Implications for Regulation." www.fda.gov/bbs/topics/NEWS/ephedra/whitepaper/html (accessed October 15, 2003).

U.S. Food and Drug Administration, Center for Food Safety and Applied Nutrition. 2001. "Products That Consumers Inquire About: Ephedra or Ephedrine." www.cfsan.fda.gov/~dms/ds-prod.html (accessed October 15, 2003).

OBESITY: PERSONAL OR POLITICAL?

Obesity is the new national epidemic. Some 65 percent of Americans (127 million people) are now either overweight or obese. Obesity is fostered by a combination of genetics and a range of environmental factors: lack of physical activity, over-consumption of food, and a high-calorie, high-fat diet.

Until the early 1990s, obesity was more or less ignored by public health officials. Indeed, doctors used to encourage patients to carry a bit of extra padding. Now, however, health professionals are downright alarmed not only because the incidence of obesity among adults and children is rising so rapidly but also because it is now well-understood that obesity creates health problems. Some 300,000 people in the United States die prematurely each year because of obesity, making it the second leading killer, after smoking. It increases one's chance of developing a whole host of medical problems including cancer, heart disease, stroke, Type 2 diabetes, high blood pressure, gallbladder disease, arthritis, and asthma.

Obesity is not just an issue for the United States. Obesity rates are mushrooming in developed and underdeveloped nations alike, affecting upward of 300 million people worldwide in 2000. The World Health Organization has called obesity "one of today's most blatantly visible—yet most neglected—public health problems." "If immediate action is not taken," says WHO, "millions will suffer from an array of serious health disorders." (Paradoxically, the obesity epidemic coexists with widespread hunger and malnutrition. According to the Food and Agriculture Organization, there are some 800 million chronically hungry people in the world [Food and Agriculture Organization 2000]).

Based on this information, many people view obesity as a public health emergency that requires some kind of coordinated government response. Although a large measure of personal responsibility and willpower must certainly come into play, obesity must also be tackled as a social and even political problem. The environmental factors that might be influenced culturally include our love affair with the automobile (and subsequent lack of biking and walking paths in most cities), excessive time in front of the television, more sedentary kinds of work (e.g., sitting in front of a computer all day), and the promotion of poor eating habits by a profit-driven food industry.

The food industry, in particular, has come under attack from health activists and professionals. Some believe that the heavy advertising of sugar cereals, soda pop, and Lunchables to kids is clear evidence that selling cheap food at a healthy profit is more important to food manufacturers than promoting health among our nation's children. Children do not make a rational choice to eat chocolate brownie cereal; they are influenced by what they see on television, by the bright packaging, by the magic elves who make the cereal in their tree-stump kitchens. Adults, too, are unduly influenced by advertising. When the cereal company says that the brownie bits provide 12 essential nutrients, this sounds like good food for the children you love. Since the industry will not self-regulate, it is up to the government and, especially, the consumer, to challenge the industry's agenda.

Activist and health professional groups seek some public accountability for the quality of food that people—especially our children—are fed. In January 2004, the American Academy of Pediatrics issued a policy statement recommending that school districts restrict the sale of soft drinks. The Yale University Center for Eating and Weight Disorders argues the need to improve the quality of federal food programs, such as school lunches, which are a nutritional disaster. On the school lunch menu this week: pizza, fish sticks, chicken nuggets, hamburgers with fries and a cookie (and ketchup, which is the vegetable of choice for American children). You have to buy your own soda from the large Coca-Cola vending machine on the east wall. Books like *Fast Food Nation, Fat Land,* and *Food Fight* try to expose the more sinister side of food.

Legislative measures may also be introduced. The Center for Science in the Public Interest is urging the government to introduce "junk food taxes"—a small tax on soda, candy, and other junk food. The revenue would be directed into nutritional education programs. Food-labeling laws might also be strengthened so that foods containing trans fats are clearly marked and health claims are strictly controlled. (Trans fats, also called partially hydrogenated fats, are formed when hydrogen atoms are added to a liquid fat in order to make it solid and increase its shelf life. Trans fats increase levels of LDL ["bad"] cholesterol and increase the risk of heart disease.) The government might also offer less extensive subsidies for sugar and meat producers.

However, there are those who believe that obesity is a wholly personal issue—that it should not be up to the government to regulate what people eat. They think that people are fat because they lack control, or simply because they like fatty food, dislike exercise, and are willing to live with the consequences. Some of those arguing this line are in the food business. They fear costly and burdensome regulations (such as strict nutrition labeling) and worry about the possibility that people will hold the food industry liable for their personal problems. Just as smokers have been successful in bringing class action lawsuits against the tobacco industry, the obese may be able to sue McDonald's.

And lest you think such lawsuits may be too far-fetched, consider the as yet unsuccessful ones against food makers. In the most well-known case, two obese teenagers from New York sued the McDonald's corporation because they said it directly caused them to become fat. The suit was eventually thrown out, but it made the food industry nervous. McDonald's argued that it handles nutrition responsibly because it hangs posters on the wall listing the fat and calorie content of menu items.

But the notion that consumers can somehow blame the industry for their own lack of willpower is unsettling. And in a litigious culture such as ours, there may well be a rash of similar attempts to lay blame on the food industry. To counter such attempts, a few legislative bills have been introduced. Both the Commonsense Consumption Act and the Personal Responsibility in Food

Consumption Act would protect the food industry from lawsuits based on an alleged injury from obesity.

Some critics of government regulation argue that unlike tobacco, which is chemically addictive, food is a matter of choice. The power of advertising does not negate personal autonomy. It may be that people like eating junk food—a Twinkie tastes good and is satisfying. Valuing gastronomic pleasure over health is a matter of choice.

Discussion Questions

1. Assess the analogy between food and tobacco. How is the food industry like and unlike the tobacco industry?

2. To what extent is obesity a personal responsibility, and to what extent is it the fault of others (like the food industry)?

3. Should foods marketed to children be regulated in ways that foods marketed to adults are not?

Resources

American Academy of Pediatrics. 2004. "News Release: AAP Says Soft Drinks in Schools Should be Restricted." www.aap.org/advocacy/releases/jansoftdrinks.htm (accessed January 8, 2004).

American Obesity Association. www.obesity.org (accessed January 7, 2004).

Associated Press. 2003. "Waists, Debate Over Fat Growing." *Daily Times-Call*, August 25, A1.

BROWNELL, KELLY, and KATHERINE BATTLE HORGEN. 2003. *Food Fight: The Inside Story of the Food Industry, America's Obesity Crisis, and What We Can Do about It.* New York: McGraw-Hill/Contemporary Books.

CRISTER, GREG. 2003. *Fat Land: How Americans Became the Fattest People in the World*. Boston: Mariner/Houghton Mifflin.

Food and Agriculture Organization. 2000. *The State of Food Insecurity in the World* 2nd ed. www.fao.org/DOCREP/X8200E/x8200e03.htm#P0_0 (accessed June 8, 2004).

SCHLOSSER, ERIC. 2001. *Fast Food Nation: The Dark Side of the All-American Meal*. Boston: Houghton Mifflin.

Surgeon General of the United States. 2003. *Surgeon General's Call to Action to Prevent and Decrease Overweight and Obesity*. www.surgeongeneral. gov/topics/obesity/calltoaction/ (accessed January 7, 2004).

World Health Organization. 2003. "Controlling the Global Obesity Epidemic." www.who.int/nut/obs.htm (accessed January 8, 2004).

ZERNIKE, KATE. 2003. "Is Obesity the Responsibility of the Body Politic?" *New York Times*, November 9, WK3.

WORRIED ABOUT HARRY POTTER

Angie Haney, a single mother of two living in Van Buren, Arkansas, was worried—about Harry Potter. She first became concerned when her pastor talked about the books at a Wednesday night church meeting. She knew that her kids had been exposed to the whole Potter buzz. But when she found out that her children's school offered extra-credit points for students who read the books, she knew she had to act. According to Haney, the Harry Potter books promote witchcraft. They also teach children to defy authority, to break school rules, and to think of parents and teachers as the enemy. Haney asked the Cedarville school board to remove the books from the school library. In June 2002, the board voted 3-2 to restrict access to the Potter series so that children would be required to have written parental permission to read the books.

A number of Christian groups have spoken out against the Potter series, claiming the books serve as an introduction to witchcraft and the occult. Tom Hess notes, as evidence, that author J. K. Rowling relies on real figures such as Nicolas Flamel, a twelfth-century French alchemist who concocted a substance known as the Philosopher's Stone, which turned base metals into silver and gold and bestowed on its creator eternal life. According to another concerned parent, "All 19 points of witchcraft are contained in these books."

The backlash to the school board's decision was swift and strong. The parents of Dakota Counts, a fourth-grader at Cedarville Elementary, filed a lawsuit in federal court in July 2002 challenging the school board's restriction. The American Booksellers Foundation for Free Expression and 13 other organizations filed an amicus brief, in which they argued, "The board's decision to censor these excellent books tramples on students' fundamental right to receive information and ideas."

According to the American Library Association, the Harry Potter books have been the most frequently challenged books in the country over the past four years. In addition to attempting to ban the books from library shelves, Christians have resisted Potter in other ways. For example, the Arkansas Baptist State Convention passed a resolution asking Baptists to protest the sale of Potter books. A group called the Jesus Party meets yearly to cut up books from the Potter series. And a church in western Pennsylvania held an old-fashioned book burning for the Potter series (also throwing into the flames several Disney videos, including *Pinocchio* and *Hercules*, and CDs by REM and Pearl Jam).

In September 2002, a judge ordered the Potter books back on the shelves at Cedarville Elementary. The first legal challenge to a restriction on the use of Harry Potter books in the public schools had been successful.

Discussion Questions

1. Should any books be banned from school libraries? How should the line be drawn?

2. Is it possible to distinguish between legitimate religious beliefs and illegifimate ones?

3. Compare this case to the argument over creationism vs. evolution in the schools.

Resources

Focus on the Family. 2004. "Harry Potter." www.family.org/topics/ A0026480.cfm (accessed June 8, 2004).

American Library Association. 2002. "Harry Potter Series Tops List of Most Challenged Books for Third Year in a Row." www.ala.org (accessed January 13, 2004).

HESS, TOM. 2002. "Putting Harry in His Place," *Citizen Magazine*. www.family.org/forum/citizenmag.

MILL, JOHN STUART. 1859. *On Liberty*. Reprinted 1988. New York: Penguin Books. See especially chapter II, "Of the Liberty of Thought and Discussion."

WAL-MART KEEPS ITS SHELVES CLEAN

Sam Walton opened his first store in Rogers, Arkansas, in 1962. He probably had no idea that the Wal-Mart stores would grow to be the world's largest retail business, with sales totaling $218 billion in 2002. Over 100 million shoppers fill the aisles of Wal-Mart each week in the United States, and a new mega-store opens somewhere in the country approximately every two days. The company employs 1.3 million associates worldwide. Wal-Mart downplays its success and expansion, claiming to be just a family store with good ole' family values.

With its open embrace of family values, it is no surprise that Wal-Mart tries to keep its shelves clean. When customers complain about items they find offensive, Wal-Mart listens—which is presumably why it routinely censors music labels and content. Wal-Mart will not stock any album bearing a parental advisory sticker, nor will it carry CDs with lyrics or cover art that is overly sexual. It will also refuse to sell music with lyrics or images about homosexuality, satanism, and abortion.

This places recording artists in a bind: Do they sanitize their art to make it palatable to Wal-Mart, or do they refuse to alter their music, with a large potential loss of sales? Wal-Mart is the world's largest CD retailer and controls about 10 percent of the total domestic music sales. Many artists have refused to change their music. Sheryl Crow, for example, refused to edit a line in which she sings, "Watch our children as they kill each other with a gun they bought at Wal-Mart discount stores." Wal-Mart is the nation's largest gun retailer. It does not sell Sheryl Crow's CD.

For the most part, recording artists will change a picture or alter a lyric in exchange for a spot on the shelves. Nirvana, for example, removed images of fetuses from the back of its *In Utero* album and changed the title of their song "Rape Me" to "Waif Me." White Zombie added little blue bikinis to cover a naked model on the cover of an album. A picture of Jesus was airbrushed off the cover of a John Mellencamp album. In fact, it has become customary for record companies to produce two versions of each album for big-name artists: the regular version and the sanitized Wal-Mart version.

Wal-Mart's policies have raised the ire of many people. Critics of the store claim that by censoring music, it is forcing people to accept Wal-Mart Brand standards of morality—actively shaping culture by determining the kinds of things artists can express. It is true, critics admit, that no one is forced to accept Wal-Mart's standards, but 10 percent of CD sales is a compelling reason for artists to bow to pressure. Customers, too, don't always have a choice about where to shop. For many small-town teenagers, Wal-Mart is the only place within a 60-mile radius that sells music. And given the sheer volume of product that passes through Wal-Mart stores, the company's power to shape consumer choice is enormous.

Wal-Mart's critics also accuse the store of hypocrisy. While refusing to sell albums with racy lyrics or covers, certain Wal-Marts still stock the swimsuit edition of *Sports Illustrated*. They sell Herbal Essences shampoo, the advertisements for which depict women having orgasms in the shower while they wash their hair. And while refusing to place a pregnant doll named Midge on the shelves, Wal-Mart happily stocks a full line of firearms and ammunition.

A number of individuals and anticensorship organizations like Rock Out Censorship and Parents for Rock and Rap have petitioned Wal-Mart to stop censoring music. And a number of recording artists have spoken out against censorship. David Roback of California's Mazzy Star said, "It's been proved time and time again that censorship does not have any positive social impact. It's just a bunch of off-the-wall people acting out some bizarre control thing." And Jakob Dylan of the Wallflowers argued, "The major downside is when people make music and start thinking about where it's going to be sold. When it infects the art that people are making that's when it's counterproductive" (Morse 1996).

Wal-Mart denies that any political agenda lurks behind its decisions about what products to carry. The customer is always right, and it is customers who guide decisions about which products will line the shelves. Wal-Mart argues that although it has received some criticism, an even greater number of supporters have written to say that they appreciate Wal-Mart's family-friendly policies. Wal-Mart argues that there is nothing unconstitutional about a large corporation openly endorsing Christian values and that we should appreciate that a large company seeks to respect a standard of morality in the communities it serves.

If you are interested in further research into the issue of censorship, Wal-Mart just might be able to help. It has a large online bookstore that carries a number of books about censorship. For example, the title *Censorship: Opposing Viewpoints*, by Rudolf Steiner and Bryon Stay, looks interesting. Unfortunately, the item is listed as temporarily unavailable.

Discussion Questions

1. Usually "censorship" refers to governmental action to control the content of speech or expression. Is "censorship" the right description of what Wal-Mart does? Is there such a thing as corporate censorship?

2. Is there any way to distinguish between selling things and shaping culture? Can a giant store like Wal-Mart *not* shape culture?

3. Is it a bad thing for Wal-Mart to shape culture?

4. One Wal-Mart supporter's response to critics was "If you don't like Wal-Mart, go somewhere else!" What are the strengths and weaknesses of this argument?

Resources

Federal Trade Commission. www.fcc.com.

MILL, JOHN STUART. 1859. *On Liberty.* Reprinted 1988. New York: Penguin Books. See especially chapter II, "Of the Liberty of Thought and Discussion."

MORSE, STEVE. 1996. "Up Against the Wal-Mart: Rockers and Rappers Claim Censorship." *Boston Globe,* December 6, C13. Also available at www.massmic.com/walmart.html.

Public Broadcasting Service. 2003. "Store Wars: When Wal-Mart Comes to Town." www.pbs.org/itvs/storewars (accessed July 23, 2003).

Wal-Mart Stores. www.walmartstores.com.

EDWARD "NJ WEEDMAN" FORCHION: GANJA BRINGS HIM CLOSER TO GOD

"The AmeriKKKan war on drugs is really a war on 'US.' The use of stimulants is part of human nature but what has occurred in 'AMERICA' is the White majority has made the substances used by 'minorities' illegal while allowing the substances used by whites; [sic] to be legal." Alcohol and cigarettes are legal, though they kill thousands of people a year. Yet marijuana, which has "killed no-one ever," is classified as a dangerous and illegal drug.

"For thousands of years Africans have used marijuana as a medicine and as 'sacraments' in native religions." Thus argues Edward "NJ Weedman" Forchion.

Edward Forchion is an unabashed advocate of marijuana, both its use and its legalization. He has run for public office several times on the Legalize Marijuana Party ticket and makes it a point to smoke the weed in front of public officials. In 2000, Forchion was convicted of possession with intent to distribute marijuana and was sentenced to 10 years in prison for brokering a drug deal for his brother involving some 40 pounds of pot. During his trial, he served as his own lawyer, calling marijuana laws unjust and asking jurors to invoke jury nullification. (In jury nullification, the jury decides to acquit a defendant even though his or her act was against the law, because the jury believes that the law is unjust or that the defendant does not deserve punishment for breaking the law.)

Forchion's central argument for legalization is a religious one: Native African religions rely on the herb for sacramental purposes. For example, Forchion's own religion, Rastafarianism, involves the ritualistic use of marijuana, or ganja, which is thought to raise partakers above the mundane and to thereby enhance spiritual unity with God and with the community of believers. Ganja is the sacred "tree of life."

According to Forchion, the war on drugs is at least partly religiously motivated, with conservative Christians seeing marijuana use (but not, presumably, the use of tobacco) as evil. Forchion tries to argue with Christian opposition to marijuana on their own grounds. Forchion's Web site includes a reference to the "holy herb": "And God said, Behold, Let the earth bring forth grass, the herb yielding seed, and the fruit tree yielding fruit after his kind, whose seed is itself, upon the earth. . . . And God saw that it was good."

Forchion served 16 months in jail and was given 27 months of intensive supervised parole for his 2000 conviction of possession with intent to distribute. However, he was sent back to prison shortly after being released on parole, for allegedly violating the rules of New Jersey's intensive supervised parole program. Among his violations: speaking to the media about marijuana legalization, creating a Web site, and filming several television commercials calling for legalization of cannabis. On January 24, 2003, the state of New Jersey was finally ordered to release Forchion. The judge ruled that Forchion's incarceration was a constitutional violation of his right to free speech and that he has the right to advocate a change in marijuana laws.

Forchion describes his actions as civil disobedience and aligns himself with one of the great civil rights activists in American history, Martin Luther King, Jr. One of the final entries on Forchion's extensive Web site is a quote from Martin Luther King, Jr., "One who breaks an unjust law must do so openly, lovingly, and with a willingness to accept the penalty. I submit that an individual who breaks a law that conscience tells him is unjust and who willingly accepts the penalty of imprisonment in order to arouse the conscience of the community over its injustice, is in reality expressing the highest respect for the law."

Discussion Questions

1. Should marijuana be legalized?

2. While marijuana continues to be illegal, should there be a religious exemption for marijuana use?

3. Are current marijuana laws racist?

Resources

BOURIE, MARK. 2003. *Hemp: A Short History of the Most Misunderstood Plant and Its Uses and Abuses.* Buffalo, NY: Firefly Books.

EDWARDS, JIM. 2003. "NJ Weedman Wins Right to Advocate Drug-Law Reform." *New Jersey Law Journal*, posted at *Cannabis News*. www.cannabisnews.com/news/thread15336.shtml (accessed October 8, 2003).

Forchion's Web site. www.njweedman.com (accessed October 8, 2003).
ROBINSON, ROWAN. 1996. *The Great Book of Hemp*. Rochester, VT: Park
    Street Press.

LICENSE-PLATE LIBERTIES

The ACLU and Planned Parenthood filed suit in Nashville over
the state's plan to issue "Choose Life" license plates. According
to the lawsuit, the plates violate the constitution because there
are no alternative plates expressing the pro-choice viewpoint.
Similar legislation is pending in several other states.

Discussion Questions

1. Does allowing states to license "Choose Life" plates
   constitute a violation of free speech?

2. Is it unethical to allow "Choose Life" plates?

Resources

Associated Press. 2003. "Tennessee: 'Choose Life' Plates Opposed." *New York
    Times*, November 8, A10.
Choose Life, Inc. www.choose-life.org.
LITHWICK, DAHLIA. 2003. "Poetic Licenses." *Slate*. http://slate.msn.com/
    id/2078247 (accessed January 13, 2004).

PLEDGE OF ALLEGIANCE

I pledge allegiance to the flag of the United States of America,
And to the Republic for which it stands.
One Nation under God, indivisible,
With Liberty and Justice for all.

Every morning, all around the country, children stand in school classrooms, facing a flag, right hand over heart, and recite these words. But will all children be reciting this pledge? Or will some sit quietly at their desk and contemplate other things? Will the children be reciting the Pledge with two words ("under God") missing? The Pledge of Allegiance has become a battlefield. At issue: patriotism, history, and religious liberty.

On October 12, 1892, as part of the National Public School Celebration of Columbus Day and by proclamation of President Harrison, the Pledge of Allegiance was first recited in schools around the country. The Pledge had been published a month earlier in a magazine for children called *Youth's Companion* and was also sent out in leaflet form to 12 million public school children.

The original Pledge was composed by Francis Bellamy, a Baptist minister and socialist, and in its original wording read:

> I pledge allegiance to my Flag,
> And to the Republic for which it stands:
> One Nation indivisible,
> With Liberty and Justice for all.

In 1923, the words "the flag of the United States" were substituted for "my flag," just in case some foreign-born children might be thinking of their homeland flag during recitation of the Pledge. In 1924, "of America" was added, just to be absolutely certain. Then in 1954, the two words were added that are now causing so much strife. According to President Eisenhower, who approved adding the words "under God," "in this way we are reaffirming the transcendence of religious faith in America's heritage and future; in this way we shall constantly strengthen those spiritual weapons which forever will be our country's most powerful resource in peace and war" (FlagDay 2003).

In the summer of 2002, the 9th Circuit Court of Appeals (which covers California, Oregon, Washington, Hawaii, Alaska, Arizona, Nevada, Montana, and Idaho) ruled that the Pledge is unconstitutional because of the words "under God"—which represent a governmental endorsement of religion. The case was brought by Michael Newdow, a father in California who did not want his daughter forced to recite the words "under God." He explained that because he is an atheist, it is offensive to him for his child to have to pledge her allegiance to God.

Although he is accused of being unpatriotic, Newdow believes that he is actually defending the Constitution by insisting on the separation of church and state. When public school children are required to recite the pledge, religion is being forced upon them. The words "under God" clearly endorse the idea that this is a Christian nation and (as Eisenhower's words suggest) that God is somehow part of our national identity. The Pledge is supposed to be unifying, but not all citizens accept the same religious tenets.

Critics of the 9th Circuit Court called the ruling ridiculous—political correctness run amok. The words "under God" are not meant to exclude anyone; they simply reflect the historical development of America as a largely Christian nation. So do a number of other "God" references, such as the "In God We Trust" on pennies, nickels, dimes, quarters, and bills. The Supreme Court begins each session with "God save the United States and this honorable court."

The ruling by the 9th Circuit Court was blasted in Congress. The Senate passed a resolution by a 99-0 vote to express support for the Pledge. The Pledge Protection Act has been introduced into the House of Representatives. The bill would prohibit lower courts from ruling that the Pledge is unconstitutional. The U.S. Supreme Court overturned the Newdow case for unrelated reasons.

Discussion Questions

1. Is it unconstitutional to require children to recite the Pledge in its current form?

2. Should the Pledge be again revised, with "under God" deleted?

3. Is this a case of "political correctness run amok"?

4. Are the words "under God" a historical reference or an endorsement of religion?

5. Might the reference to "God" exclude even religious people, such as the Muslim child who might use Allah or the Jewish child who might use Yahweh?

Resources

BAER, JOHN W. 1992. "The Pledge of Allegiance, a Short History." http://history.vineyard.net/pledge.htm.
CNN.com./Law Center. 2002. "Lawmakers Blast Pledge Ruling." June 27. www.cnn.com/2002/LAW/06/26/pledge.allegiance/(accessed November 13, 2003).
FLAGDAY. 2003. "The Story of the Pledge of Allegiance." http://flagday.org.Pages/StoryofPledge.html (accessed November 13, 2003).
MORAHAN, LAWRENCE. 2003. "Lawmakers Line Up Behind Pledge of Allegiance." *CNSNews.com,* June 19. www.cnsnews.com/ViewPolitics.asp?Page=\Politics\archive\200306\POL20030619d.html (accessed November 14, 2003).
Restore Our Pledge. www.restorethepledge.com/.

ED ROSENTHAL AND MEDICAL MARIJUANA

Should marijuana be legalized for medical use? Many, including Ed Rosenthal, would argue a resounding yes. Rosenthal, arrested in 2002 for growing pot, has been at the center of an intense fight over the medical use of marijuana. Although his cannabis crop was legal according to California law—in 1996 voters passed the California Compassionate Use Act, which allows individuals to legally grow marijuana for medical use—under federal drug laws, Rosenthal's crop was illegal. Although he received the most lenient sentence possible—one day in prison and a $1,000 fine—he was unhappy to have been arrested at all and vowed to intensify his crusade to make medical marijuana legal.

Hemp, or *Cannabis sativa*, has long been a vital part of the human medicinal armamentarium. Its use has been documented in early Chinese medicine, in the Ayurvedic system of India, and in early European folk remedies. As late as the end of the 19th century, cannabis was used in drugs sold by America's giant pharmaceutical companies Eli Lilly, Parke-Davis, and Squibb. Then, within the span of about 50 years, cannabis fell out of favor, at least in the West. It went from being a miracle drug to being an illegal substance.

The major cannabinoids—tetrahydrocannabinol (THC), cannabinol (CBN), and cannabidiol (CBD)—have been successfully applied to a wide range of physical ailments. They have been used to control glaucoma, an eye disease that can lead to blindness; to relieve nausea and vomiting related to chemotherapy treatments for cancer; to treat asthma, arthritis, depression, inflammation, migraines, and insomnia; and as a powerful pain reliever.

Despite volumes of reputable medical literature describing the therapeutic benefits of cannabis, it cannot presently be taken as a medicine in most of the United States. Nine states (Alaska, Arizona, California, Colorado, Hawaii, Maine, Nevada, Oregon, Washington) have medical marijuana laws making it legal for sick and dying patients to smoke, with a doctor's recommendation. Yet, under federal law, it is illegal for doctors to prescribe or even recommend the use of marijuana. This puts doctors in an awkward position: they can freely discuss its medical benefits, but they cannot actually recommend that a patient use it. "It will ease your pain and quiet your nausea, but . . ."

Some of those in favor of changing the nation's marijuana laws argue that the government should distinguish between recreational and medicinal use of the drug. Others believe that given the drug's usefulness and relative safety, any and every use of marijuana should be legal.

Discussion Questions

1. Other than its legal status, is there anything that would distinguish marijuana from other drugs prescribed by physicians?

2. Should marijuana be legalized for medicinal use?

3. Should all uses of marijuana be legal?

4. What arguments might be made against legalization of marijuana for medicinal use?

Resources

BOURRIE, MARK. 2003. *Hemp: A Short History of the Most Misunderstood Plant and Its Uses and Abuses.* Buffalo, NY: Firefly Books.
GRINSPOON, L., and J. B. BAKALAR. 1995. "Marijuana as Medicine: A Plea for Reconsideration." *Journal of the American Medical Association* 273: 1875–76.
The Marijuana Policy Project. www.mpp.org (accessed January 12, 2004).
Marijuana Web site. www.marijuana.org (accessed January 12, 2004).
MURRAY, DEAN E. 2003. "Marijuana Grower Sentenced to One Day and $1,000 Fine." *New York Times,* June 5, A22.
ROBINSON, ROWAN. 1996. *The Great Book of Hemp.* Rochester, VT: Park Street Press.
TULLER, DAVID. 2003. "Doctors Tread a Thin Line on Marijuana Advice." *New York Times,* October 28, D5.

CAMERAS WATCHING STUDENTS

After the deadly shooting at Columbine High School in the spring of 1999, schools around the country began worrying more about safety. Many have installed metal detectors at entrances, hired security guards, and installed cameras in corridors and cafeterias. But a school district in Biloxi, Mississippi, has gone so far as to install cameras in every classroom. Everything a student does and says during the day is on record. The cameras turn out to be very useful for teachers and school administrators. Was there a question about whether Johnny cheated on his history test? Who stole Susie's Cheetah Girls CD? Who was passing notes during class? Just check the videotape. Amazingly, say school officials, student behavior has improved and test scores have gone up. Aware that they are being watched, the students are careful about what they do.

But some people are troubled by the classroom surveillance system. They feel that adolescents should learn to behave because it is right, not because they feel themselves being watched—the moral censor needs to be internal. Also, even though they are adolescents, constant video surveillance is an infringement of their civil liberties. It is one thing to have school entrances and hallways monitored by video; it is another to have cameras on students at all times during the school day. Furthermore, the infringement on students' civil liberties is not justified by any real threat of violence. Looking at the statistics, we can see that although multiple-victim homicide events such as the Columbine shootings have increased in frequency, overall school violence is no worse now than it was a decade ago.

Discussion Questions

1. Are classroom cameras an infringement on students' civil liberties?

2. Is there a significant difference between video cameras in hallways and in classrooms?

3. Is the argument about internal moral sensors a reasonable one?

Resources

DILLON, SAM. 2003. "Cameras Watching Students, Especially in Biloxi." *New York Times*, September 24, A23.
ORWELL, GEORGE. 1949. *1984*. New York: Everyman's Library, 1992 reissue.

HIGH SCHOOL TELLS STUDENT TO REMOVE ANTI-WAR SHIRT

On February 17, 2003, Bretton Barber was sent home from school early. His offense: wearing a T-shirt with a picture of President George Bush framed with the words "INTERNATIONAL TERRORIST." The school's vice principal asked Bretton to turn his shirt inside out, and when Bretton refused he was asked to leave school for the rest of the day. Bretton's justification: "I wore the T-shirt to express my anti-war sentiment." The vice principal's justification: students are not allowed to wear shirts that promote terrorism. It is unclear what the vice principal meant: did he believe that the T-shirt would provoke a violent conflict at the school, or did he find its message politically incorrect (being against Bush is equivalent to promoting terrorism)?

The case raised in a pointed way the question of what rights students have to express their political views at school. The Supreme Court in *Tinker v. Des Moines* (1969) ruled that the expression of political viewpoints in school cannot be prohibited unless there is evidence that it will cause a substantial disruption of education or a problem with discipline. *Tinker* revolved around the question of whether the First Amendment rights of three public school students were violated when they were suspended for wearing black armbands to protest the government's policies in Vietnam. The Court ruled that wearing an armband was a symbolic act, aimed to express a certain opinion. Symbolic acts are a form of speech protected under the First Amendment. The Court ruled, "It can hardly be argued that either students or teachers shed their constitutional rights to freedom of speech or expression at the schoolhouse gate."

Still, the Court also recognized that there may be a conflict between students' exercise of free speech and the rules of school authorities. School authorities have far greater ability to restrict students' expression than the government has in restricting the expression of its citizens. In such conflict, there must be a balance.

The district court had upheld the school's action to prohibit the wearing of armbands, for fear that there would be a disturbance. According to the Supreme Court, however, "fear or apprehension of a disturbance is not enough to overcome the right to freedom of expression." Justice Brennan, speaking for the Court in an earlier case, wrote: "The Nation's future depends upon leaders trained through wide exposure to that robust exchange of idea which discovers truth 'out of a multitude of tongues,' [rather] than through any kind of authoritative selection" (*Keyishian v. Board of Regents* 1967).

Justice Black, in his dissenting opinion, questioned the idea that freedom of speech can be exercised "at a whim," any place and anywhere. He wrote, ". . . if the time has come when pupils of state-supported schools, kindergartens, grammar schools, or high schools can defy and flout orders of school officials to keep their minds on their own schoolwork, it is the beginning of a new revolutionary era of permissiveness in the country fostered by the judiciary."

Discussion Questions

1. Were Bretton's free speech rights violated by his school?

2. Just how volatile a piece of clothing is Bretton's T-shirt?

3. Bretton's wearing of an anti-war shirt did not seem to interfere with the orderly conduct of his school. Given this, would the school be justified in asking him to turn his shirt inside out or leave school?

4. What do you make of the vice principal's concern that Bretton's shirt "supported terrorism"?

5. Is there any cutoff age at which children should be considered not to have First Amendment rights?

6. Should the speech rights of students gradually increase as they get older?

Resources

Keyishian et al. v. Board of Regents of the University of the State of New York et al., 385 U.S. 589 (1967).

JOHNSON, JOHN. W. 1998. *The Struggle for Student Rights: Tinker v. Des Moines and the 1960s.* Lawrence: University of Kansas Press.

LEWIN, TAMAR. 2003. "High School Tells Student to Remove Antiwar Shirt." *New York Times*, February 26, A12.

Tinker et al. v. Des Moines Independent Community School District et al., 393 U.S. 503 (1969).

CRACK—GET STERILIZED, GET CASH

Imagine being paid $200 not to get pregnant! All you have to do is sign a contract agreeing to get long-term birth control and, as soon as you provide proof that you've had the tubal ligation or the Depo-Provera injections, the cash is yours. No, this is not an Internet promotion from a pharmaceutical company, nor is it a rebate offer. This cash-for-sterilization plan is the brainchild of Project Prevention: Children Requiring a Caring Kommunity (CRACK). Project Prevention was started in Anaheim, California, in 1997 by a woman named Barbara Harris. After adopting four children from the same drug-addicted woman, Harris felt she had to do something to address the crisis of children being born to drug-addicted parents. Her small effort has been to prevent what unwanted pregnancies she can by offering a reward for the drug-addicted man or woman who chooses birth control over pregnancy. There is no stated rule that one must be a drug addict to participate in the cash-for-sterilization program, but Harris and her group target addicts by hanging flyers in neighborhoods known for drug problems and by coordinating with parole officers, social workers, and drug treatment programs.

"Our main objective," says Project Prevention, "is to offer effective preventive measures to reduce the tragedy of numerous drug-affected pregnancies." Unlike some programs that seek to reduce drug-addict pregnancies by incarcerating women for their drug habit (for example, by arresting them in the hospital after they have given birth), Project Prevention says that it does not punish the drug addict. Indeed, it doesn't even tell the addict what to do with the $200 cash reward—it may even be spent on more drugs. Participation in the program is completely voluntary. While its largest influence is still in southern California, Project Prevention has begun programs in Chicago and New York.

Since its inception, Project Prevention has been subject to harsh criticism. Some critics describe the program as a not-so-subtle form of eugenics—making sure that the wrong kind of people are not having babies. It also smacks of racism: Most of the people targeted by the program are black. Furthermore, offering money to an addict is a nasty form of coercion; someone high on drugs cannot make informed choices about her or his reproductive future. Project Prevention will not give $200 for short-term birth control—only for methods that are irreversible or very long term.

One of the groups opposed to the spread of Project Prevention is New York–based National Advocates for Pregnant Women. The executive director writes that "the greatest threat to

America today is not drugs and it is not their parents who may or may not use drugs" but, rather, the fact that so many people are without health care, housing, and drug treatment. The Campaign for Tobacco Free Kids in New York also voiced opposition to Project Prevention, saying that tobacco use poses a far more significant threat to the unborn than crack cocaine does.

Discussion Questions

1. Is the cash-for-sterilization program unethical?

2. Can a drug addict make an informed choice about birth control? Is an uninformed choice better than doing nothing to control one's reproductive future?

3. Assess the argument of the National Advocates for Pregnant Women.

4. Now assess the argument of the Campaign for Tobacco Free Kids.

Resources

National Advocates for Pregnant Women. 2002. "Controversial 'cash-for-sterilization' California Group Comes to New York." www.advocatesforpregnantwomen.org/issues/crackprotest.htm (accessed January 9, 2004).

Project Prevention Web site. 2004. http://cashforbirthcontrol.com/ (accessed January 9, 2004).

VEGA, CECILIA. 2003. "Cash-for-Sterilization Plan Starts Slowly in New York." *New York Times*, January 6. (Also see www.nytimes.com/2003/01/06/nyregion/06CRAC.html.)

MY HUMMER, MY CHOICE

From two Letters to the Editor:

> I found "My life, My Hummer" (*Escapes*, Sept. 26) fascinating and terrifying. Karen Strickland wonders, seemingly without guile, why pesky do-gooders might resent her passion for driving an H2. How about this: the beast, as she lovingly calls it, not only pollutes the air and wastes fuel (fostering our dependence on foreign oil), but also turns the old-fashioned highway fender-bender into a deadly catastrophe.
>
> She says, "If I don't have the freedom to decide what's good for me, then maybe we have the wrong country right now." I say that with rights come responsibilities."
>
> —Steven Cutler, New York,
> *New York Times*, Sept. 27, 2003

> Of course Karen Strickland has the right to buy and drive her Hummer. The trouble is that the price of gasoline in the United States doesn't reflect the true cost of the damage her choice causes. . . . If Hummer owners paid their proportionate share of these [environmental, health, and air quality] costs, instead of leaving them for our children to pay, I'd be happier with their freedom to choose.
>
> —Cathie Murray, Hallowel, Maine,
> *New York Times*, Sept. 26, 2003

Discussion Questions

1. What conception of justice is assumed by Murray in her comments?

2. Is it the same conception of justice assumed by Cutler in his remarks?

3. What might we imagine in Karen Strickland's conception of justice, as she argues in defense of her Hummer habit?

4. Is it irresponsible to drive a Hummer? If so, what other vehicles might it be irresponsible to drive?

5. According to Murray's logic, wouldn't *any* vehicle be problematic to drive?

6. Do people have an unencumbered right to consume? What might constrain this right?

Resources

BRADSHER, KEITH. 2002. *High and Mighty: SUVs—The World's Most Dangerous Vehicles and How They Got That Way.* New York: PublicAffairs.

DE GRAAF, JOHN, DAVID WAAN, and THOMAS H. NAYLOR. 2001. *Affluenza: The All-Consuming Epidemic.* San Francisco: Berrett-Koehler.

"My Hummer, Myself: And the Rest of Us?" 2003. Letters to the Editor of the *New York Times.* October 1, A26.

"LET THOSE WHO RIDE DECIDE": MOTORCYCLE HELMET LAWS AND BIKER RIGHTS

"On a motorcycle, the border between dangerous stupidity and the pursuit of happiness can blur to the vanishing point," writes motorcyclist Alex Berenson. "Whatever their personal politics, motorcyclists instinctively understand that the freedom to make decisions must sometimes extend to the freedom to make bad ones, in the pursuit of liberty or love or even speed."

Motorcycles are all about freedom, about the wind whipping against your face and through your hair. And mandatory helmet laws, which are in place in many states, take away this freedom. Sure, there is evidence that wearing a helmet provides protection against serious head injury and death during a crash. But motorcycles are not, essentially, about safety. They are about freedom. Helmet-wearing, say cyclists, should be a personal choice.

For those in favor of mandatory helmet laws, the issue is not merely one of individual rights. These individuals live in society— and the rest of us happen to pick up the pieces when a motorcyclist goes down. For those motorcyclists who are uninsured, society pays hospital bills, unemployment benefits, and perhaps long-term care. So society in fact has a very strong interest in whether or not the risk of severe injury is reduced through helmet use. And indeed, study after study has shown that wearing a helmet dramatically reduces the chances of severe head injury during a crash.

In 2001, the American College of Surgeons (ACS), who see many motorcycle crash victims, issued a statement in support of helmet laws. According to ACS, "Helmeted motorcycle riders have up to an 85 percent reduced incidence of severe, serious, and critical brain injuries compared with unhelmeted riders." The average inpatient hospital costs for riders with severe head injury are nearly double those of riders without head injury.

Bikers respond that risk-taking cannot be viewed as inherently bad. Indeed, many of the activities that people feel most passionate about contain an element of risk: skydiving, rock climbing, scuba diving. And many more-mundane activities— driving to work, smoking a cigarette, walking down the stairs— are somewhat risky, too. Taxes not only pay for motorcyclists' injuries but also cover the health costs of those who smoke, overeat, and don't exercise. Why pick on bikers?

Discussion Questions

1. Should helmets be mandatory for motorcyclists?

2. Do helmet laws unfairly target bikers?

3. In what circumstances and to what degree should society pick up the pieces for people who take risks?

Resources

American College of Surgeons. 2001. "Statement in Support of Motorcycle Helmet Laws." *Bulletin of the American College of Surgeons* 86 (2).
BERENSON, ALEX. 2003. "Born to Be Wild, but at a Cost." *New York Times,* July 6, WK5.
Biker Rights Online. 2004. "Helmet Issues." www.bikersrights.com/helmets. html (accessed January 12, 2004).
Insurance Institute for Highway Safety-Highway Loss Data Institute. 2003. "Q & A: Motorcycle Helmet Use Laws." www.hwysafety.org/ safety_facts/qanda/helmet_use/htm (accessed January 12, 2004).
Lonebiker Web site. www.lonebiker.com (accessed June 8, 2004).

USA PATRIOT ACT

Six weeks after the September 11 terrorist attacks on the United States, when the nation was still in shock, with minimal debate Congress hastily passed legislation called "United and Strengthening America by Providing Tools Required to Intercept and Obstruct Terrorism"—what is now known by its acronym, the USA Patriot Act. The Justice Department argues that the increased law enforcement powers provided by the Patriot Act are necessary to effectively interdict terrorist organizations.

Some of the key provisions of the act include

- Sneak and peek searches (Sec. 213). Allow the government to search an individual's private property without telling the person beforehand.

- PEN register and trap and trace searches (Sec. 214). Allow law enforcement to trace "addressing" information of communications (e.g., subject lines in e-mail letters, URLs for Web pages).

- Access to records under FISA, the Foreign Intelligence Surveillance Act (Sec. 215). Allows the FBI to order any person or entity to turn over "any tangible things" as long as the order is for an "authorized investigation." The FBI could access library, computer, medical, student, Internet service provider, and credit card records.

- A broadened definition of terrorism to include "domestic terrorism."

The strength of the Patriot Act is that it attempts to increase governmental power to thwart terrorism. Civil liberties groups have objected strenuously to the increased governmental power to keep tabs on people, even if doing so can prevent future attacks.

The American Civil Liberties Union (ACLU) has been on the front lines of the battle against the Patriot Act. The ACLU writes, "Anti-terrorism policies that infringe on basic rights—such as ethnically based roundups of innocent persons, or intrusive surveillance of peaceful political activists—not only make America less free, they make our nation more vulnerable to terrorism. Such policies waste scarce government resources that should be used to track down real criminals, and help sew the seeds of mistrust among communities that might otherwise be willing to assist the government in arresting terrorists" (American Civil Liberties Union 2003).

Specifically, the ACLU argues that Section 215, expanding the government's ability to spy on its own citizens, is in direct violation of the Fourth Amendment (reasonable search and seizure) because it allows a search without warrant. It allows the FBI, for example, to demand library records for a patron. It violates the First Amendment because it prohibits those served with Section 215 orders (e.g., the library) from disclosing this information to anyone else (e.g., the person whose records were requested). The government can get information about you without your ever knowing it did so.

According to the ACLU, secret ("sneak and peak") searches also violate the Fourth Amendment, which says that the government must announce that it will search your property before it does so. ("The right of the people to be secure in their persons, houses, papers, and effects, against unreasonable searches and seizures, shall not be violated, and no warrants shall issue, but upon probable cause, supported by oath or affirmation, and particularly describing the place to be searched, and the persons or things to be seized.") Our right to participate in civil protest is also hampered. The broadening of "terrorism" to include "domestic terrorism" means that the government can monitor the activities of protestors. The ACLU states, "The Patriot Act transforms protestors into terrorists if they engage in conduct that 'involves acts dangerous to human life' to 'influence the policy of a government by intimidation or coercion.'" Abortion activists and members of the Earth Liberation Front could both be considered terrorists, under this definition.

Discussion Questions

1. If the threat of terrorist acts against the United States has increased, does this justify the increased discretionary power of law enforcement in this country?

2. Does the Patriot Act protect American citizens? Does it erode their civil liberties? Which is more important?

3. Should the government be able to detain people indefinitely without a trial, in connection with a terrorism investigation?

Resources

American Civil Liberties Union. 2003. "How 'Patriot Act 2' Would Further Erode the Basic Checks on Government Power That Keep America Safe and Free." Posted March 20, 2003. www.aclu.org/SafeandFree/SafeandFree.cfm?ID=12161&c=206 (accessed January 10, 2004).

"Uniting and Strengthening America by Providing Appropriate Tools Required to Intercept and Obstruct Terrorism Act." October 24, 2001. H.R. 3162.

Value and Culture

Same-Sex Unions and the Defense of Marriage

Gay Sex and Adultery

Sex Education in School

Evolution vs. Creationism in Public Schools

Creationism, Take Two: Professor Dini's Recommendation

Sports Supplementation: Fair or Foul?

Sports Supplementation, Take Two: Ross Rebagliati

Extreme Makeover

Culture Wars

Bright Rights

A Call to Civil Society

Ethics for the Information Age: The SCANS Report

Character Education of Children

Character Education, Take Two: Georgia's "Respect for the Creator" Principle

Rigoberta Menchú: The Purpose of Truth

≈ SAME-SEX UNIONS AND THE DEFENSE OF MARRIAGE

Resolution 56 was introduced in the House of Representatives in 2003. The proposed "Federal Marriage Amendment" to the U.S. Constitution reads, "Marriage in the United States shall consist only of the union of a man and a woman. Neither this constitution or the constitution of any state, nor state or federal law, shall be construed to require that marital status or the legal incidents thereof be conferred upon unmarried couples or groups." Why the sudden need to write marriage into the Constitution?

Although marriage has the image of a time-honored and, in a sense, timeless tradition, how to define the institution of marriage is far from clear and uncontroversial. Indeed, the right of certain people to marry has only recently been granted: it was only after the Civil War that African Americans were allowed to marry, and interracial marriages did not obtain legal protection until 1967. Now, a cultural battle is being fought over whether a marriage must take place between a man and a woman.

The first major legal step toward same-sex marriage took place in Hawaii more than a decade ago. In 1993, the Hawaii Supreme Court ruled that the restriction of marriage to opposite-sex couples would be presumed unconstitutional unless the state could demonstrate a compelling interest in the matter. Within hours, the legislature responded by amending the law to specify that marriage must be between a man and a woman. Finally, in 1999, the Hawaii Supreme Court ruled that gays and lesbians would not be allowed to marry. Nevertheless, the court also held that denial of the protections that come with marriage is unconstitutional. The state is now left trying to figure out how to provide the civil protections that come with marriage while denying licenses to same-sex couples.

In reaction to the Hawaii events, Congress in 1996 passed the Defense of Marriage Act (DOMA), which provided that no state would be compelled to recognize a same-sex marriage from another state—allowing states the freedom to restrict marriage to opposite-sex couples. The Defense of Marriage Act is a pointed attempt to clarify existing legislation, which says that marriage is a contract between a husband and a wife, language that, without the extra clarification that husbands must be male and wives female, could be interpreted to apply to same-sex couples. More than half of the states have now enacted DOMAs banning same-sex marriage.

Such laws control only marriage; states can still create laws that cover different kinds of relationships, such as domestic partnerships and civil unions. Vermont, for example, recognizes a civil union between homosexuals or lesbians. California recognizes "domestic partnerships." Under these "civil unions," a gay couple could then be eligible for the estimated 400 state benefits granted to married couples. They would be ineligible, however, for any of the 1,000 or so federal rights and benefits conferred on married couples.

The 2003 case of *Lawrence v. Texas*, which finally struck down sodomy laws in the United States, has brought increased attention to the issue of gay unions. In *Lawrence*, the U.S. Supreme Court ruled unconstitutional a Texas law making it a crime for two people of the same sex to engage in intimate sexual acts. Justice Kennedy, writing for the majority, said, "Liberty presumes an autonomy of self that includes freedom of thought, belief, expression, and certain intimate conduct." Jeffrey Rosen wrote in the *New York Times*, "The Supreme Court in *Lawrence* did far more than strike down an extreme and discriminatory Texas law that forbade sodomy by homosexuals. The Court also overruled *Bowers v. Hardwick*, a 1986 opinion holding that moral disapproval was a legitimate reason for states to regulate intimate behavior." *Lawrence* made it considerably more likely that courts will begin to recognize a constitutional right to gay marriage.

For many of those opposed to gay marriage, the issue is not marriage so much as it is homosexuality. They think homosexuality is immoral and that to sanction it with marriage legitimates it, thereby damaging the moral fabric of our society. But homosexuality is increasingly accepted as a part of our culture. Those who argue that it is immoral are increasingly challenged by scientific research that suggests that sexual orientation is not so much chosen as predetermined by one's genetic makeup. Being gay is no longer considered a disease or spiritual failing, fixable through prayer or therapy.

Although social acceptance of homosexuality looms large in the debate over same-sex unions, the institution of marriage itself is also under discussion. Some opponents of gay marriage believe that the cultural institution of marriage is a vital element of our society and that stable married couples are the corner-stone of our society, the base from which child rearing takes place.

Stanley Kurtz, contributing editor of the *National Review Online*, argues,

> . . . [G]ay marriage is a surpassingly radical attack on the very foundations of marriage itself. It detaches marriage from the distinctive dynamics of heterosexual sexuality, divorces mar-riage from its intimate connection to the rearing of children, and opens the way to the replacement of marriage by a series of infinitely flexible contractual arrangements. . . .
>
> It is true that marriage itself, and not merely women and children, domesticates men. But my point is that marriage is only able to do so by building upon the underlying dynamic of male-female sexuality. Marriage does indeed invoke public expectations of fidelity and mutual support through ritual ges-tures like weddings. But wedding or no, the public will not condemn a man who sleeps around on another man, or who fails to support his male partner financially. A wedding embodies and reinforces already existing public sentiments about a man's responsibilities to a woman; it cannot create such sentiments out of thin air." (Kurtz 2003)

Supporters of gay marriage counter that gays, too, have stable relationships. If this is what society needs, would it not make sense, then, to allow, even encourage, homosexual couples to enter into lifelong legal relationships with each other? Furthermore, het-erosexuals are hardly perfect when it comes to stable, caring rela-tionships, and often the social challenges faced by homosexual couples ensure a much more enduring union than do the fly-by-night Vegas marriages of many men and women.

Discussion Questions

1. What is the value of marriage?

2. And do same-sex unions challenge this value in a fundamental way?

3. Is the decline of marriage itself a good or bad thing?

Resources

Alliance for Marriage. www.allianceformarriage.org/ (accessed October 29, 2003).

BAIRD, ROBERT M., and STUART E. ROSENBAUM. 1997. *Same-Sex Marriage: The Moral and Legal Debate.* Amherst, NY: Prometheus Books.

BELLUCK, PAM. 2003. "Marriage by Gays Gains Big Victory in Massachusetts." *New York Times,* November 19, A1.

FALWELL, JERRY. 2003. "The Federal Marriage Amendment." Newsmax.com.www.newsmax.com/archives/articles2003/8/7/143308.shtml (accessed October 29, 2003).

Family Research Council. www.frc.org (accessed October 29, 2003).

Freedom to Marry. www.freedomtomarry.org/ (accessed October 27, 2003).

Gay-Civil-Unions.com. 2003. "The Media Debate over Same-Sex Unions." www.gay-civil-unions.com/HTML/main.htm (accessed October 27, 2003).

KURTZ, STANLEY. 2003. "Point of No Return." *National Review Online.* www.nationalreview.com/contributers/kurtz080301.shtml (accessed October 27, 2003).

LAWRENCE et al. v. Texas. 2003. Supreme Court of the United States. No. 02-102. Decided June 26, 2003.

National Marriage Project at Rutgers University. 2003. "State of Our Unions: The Social Health of Marriage in American [sic] 2003." http://marriage.rutgets.edu (accessed October 29, 2003).

Religious Tolerance. 2003. "Homosexual (Same-Sex Marriage)—All Sides to the Issue." www.religioustolerance.org/hom_marr.htm (accessed October 27, 2003).

RUBERSTEIN, WILLIAM B., and R. BRADLEY SEARS. 2003. "Toward More Perfect Unions." *New York Times*, November 20, A33.

SULLIVAN, ANDREW, ed. 1997. *Same-Sex Marriage, Pro and Con: A Reader.* New York: Vintage Books.

GAY SEX AND ADULTERY

The New Hampshire Supreme Court ruled 3-2 in a divorce case that a sexual relationship between a married woman and another woman did not constitute adultery. Florida, Georgia, and South Carolina have defined adultery more broadly to include gay sex.

Discussion Questions

1. Which legal definition of adultery makes better sense, New Hampshire's or Florida's?

2. What would be the best moral definition of adultery?

3. Is adultery immoral? Under all circumstances?

Resources

Associated Press. 2003. "New Hampshire: The Other Woman Is No Adulterer." *New York Times*, November 8, A10.

SEX EDUCATION IN SCHOOL

The debate over sex education in the schools began in earnest in 1981, when President Reagan signed the Adolescent Family Life Act. The AFLA gave $2 million in federal money to school programs that encouraged "chastity and self-discipline" when it came to sex. Since then, a battle has been raging between those who believe that programs promoting abstinence are best for our teenagers and those who believe that school programs should offer a much more comprehensive, less morally biased, education about sex.

People involved in this debate agree that unprotected sexual intercourse is a serious public health issue for America's teenagers. Almost 50 percent of high school students report having had sex, and most of them did not use a condom. Every year, about 860,000 teenage girls become pregnant, and about 3 million teens contract a sexually transmitted disease (Centers for Disease Control 2003). Although the number of reported cases of AIDS in the United States has been declining, the rate of infection among youth has remained constant. Youth who engage in sex also experience emotional consequences, from guilt to fear to regret.

What to do about the problems of teenage sex? Some feel that teens should be discouraged from sex altogether, whereas others believe that teenagers should be helped to handle the emotional and physical aspects of their teenage sexual experiences.

Abstinence-only programs are based on the philosophy that "a mutually faithful, monogamous relationship in the context of marriage is the only appropriate setting for sexual intercourse" (language from a Mississippi law mandating abstinence-only education). Proponents of abstinence-only programs note that many teenagers want to wait until they are married—or at least older—before having sex and that they need to be given the peer support and social skills to make this choice acceptable. When we teach kids how to use condoms or other contraceptives, we are sending the message that premarital sex is appropriate. Social forces pressure kids into sexual relationships far sooner than they themselves really desire, so the emphasis in sex education must be on helping kids make the right decision about sex.

Comprehensive programs, in contrast, take what they consider to be a more expansive view, that "young people need a broad base of knowledge about sexuality to help them establish healthy, positive behaviors." This broad base includes accurate and complete information about contraception, protection against sexually transmitted diseases, and human sexual development. Comprehensive programs do emphasize abstinence as the most effective way to prevent pregnancy and disease. But they do not stop there. Teenagers will have sex—so the argument goes—and it is far better that they make informed choices about their sexuality than that they blunder along blindly, getting pregnant and contracting diseases in the process.

For now, abstinence-only programs seem to have the upper hand. According to the Alan Guttmacher Institute, 86 percent of school districts with sex education programs require that abstinence be promoted as the preferable choice. Thirty-five percent of programs require that abstinence be presented as the only appropriate option for unmarried people (Dailard 2001).

Discussion Questions

1. Should we try to suppress teen sexual behavior, or should we prepare teens as best we can to deal with sex maturely?

2. Should sex education be something that parents do or that "professionals" in school do?

3. Is it an infringement of parents' rights when sex education is part of the school curriculum?

4. Is premarital sex wrong?

Resources

CAMPOS, DAVID. 2002. *Sex, Youth, and Sex Education*. Santa Barbara, CA: ABC-CLIO.

Centers for Disease Control. 2003. "Adolescent and School Health: Health Topics, Sexual Behavior." www.cdc.gov/nccdphp/dash/sexualbehaviors/index.htm (accessed November 12, 2003).

DAILARD, CYNTHIA. 2001. "Sex Education: Politicians, Parents, Teachers and Teens." *The Guttmacher Report on Public Policy* 4, no. 1 (February). Also available at www.agi-usa.org/pubs/journals/gr040109.html (accessed November 12, 2003).

DONOVAN, PATRICIA. 1998. "School-Based Sexuality Education: The Issues and Challenges." *Family Planning Perspectives* 30 (4). Also available at www.agi-usa.org/pubs/journals/3018898.html (accessed November 12, 2003).

Focus on the Family. 2003. "Sex Education." www.family.org/pplace/topics/a0025321.cfm (accessed November 12, 2003).

GRAMCKOW, JERRY. 2003. "The Real Values Behind 'Values-Free' Sex Education." www.family.org/cforum/fosi/purity/education/a0026948.cfm (accessed November 12, 2003).

IRVINE, JANICE M. 2002. *Talk about Sex: The Battles over Sex Education in the United States*. Berkeley: University of California Press.

LEVINE, JUDITH, and JOYCELYN M. ELDERS. 2002. *Harmful to Minors: The Perils of Protecting Children from Sex*. Minneapolis: University of Minnesota Press.

Sexuality Information and Education Council of the United States. www.siecus.org/school/sex_ed/mandate/mand0000.html. 2001. (accessed November 12, 2003).

WHITEHEAD, BARBARA DAFOE. 1994. "The Failure of Sex Education." *Atlantic Monthly*, 274, no. 4 (Ootober): 55.

EVOLUTION VS. CREATIONISM IN PUBLIC SCHOOLS

Evolution: Life on earth has evolved from its earliest origins through natural selection and environmental change into the diversity of species alive today. Based on radioactive dating, scientists estimate the origins of the earth to be about 4.6 billion years ago. Based on the fossil record and other data, life is currently thought to have arisen about 3.7 billion years ago.

Creationism: God put all living creatures on earth as they are today. Based on biblical genealogies, creationists believe that the earth is about 6,000 years old. A great flood is responsible for its present form.

Intelligent design: The diversity of life on earth cannot be explained by evolution but reflects the purposeful scheme of a higher power. The earth may be 4.6 billion years old, but only divine guidance could have evolved life.

The term *theistic evolution* is sometimes used to refer to the belief that God created the universe and the various processes that drive evolution. The complexity of life, which science helps us see and understand, reflects the wonder of God's creation.

The so-called Scopes monkey trial of 1925 marks the beginning of the legal controversy over creationism and evolution in U.S. public schools (though the philosophical battle between theology and science is obviously much older). The trial of *John Scopes v. State of Tennessee* was actually contrived: the American Civil Liberties Union sought someone to challenge a Tennessee statute passed in March 1925 that prohibited the teaching in public schools of theories contrary to the accepted biblical account of man's creation. Scopes, a 24-year-old biology teacher and football coach, offered to test the law in court. Clarence Darrow, arguing for the defense, claimed that the Tennessee statute violated the First Amendment separation of church and state. Scopes was convicted of teaching the theory of evolution and was fined $100, though the charges against him were eventually dropped on a technicality. The law was finally repealed in 1967.

It wasn't until 1968, in the case of *Epperson v. Arkansas*, that the U.S. Supreme Court ruled that prohibiting the teaching of evolution was unconstitutional. By the turn of the twenty-first

century, a series of cases had established that public school curriculum cannot restrict the teaching of evolution and cannot
require that creationism be taught alongside evolution.

Yet the battle is far from over. And although science may have
been a temporary victor, creationism seems to be making something of a comeback. Several states are now teaching creationism,
either outright or simply through neglect of evolution. For example, in August 1999, the Kansas Board of Education decided to
delete mention of evolution from the school science curriculum.
The decision does not forbid the teaching of evolution; it simply
does not require it. In September 2002, the Cobb County Board of
Education in Georgia approved a policy that allows teachers to
introduce differing theories about the origins of life. Alabama and
Arkansas require every science textbook to have a disclaimer
pasted on the front that reminds students that evolution is theory,
not fact. According to a report from the Fordham Foundation, 12
states currently teach almost nothing about evolution in their science curriculum.

The First Amendment to the U.S. Constitution guarantees
religious freedom to all citizens: "Congress shall make no law
respecting the establishment of religion, or prohibiting the free
exercise thereof." In the context of public education, the first half
of this amendment, known as the establishment clause, forbids
schools to endorse a particular religious doctrine or activity; the
second half, the free exercise clause, establishes the rights of students to express their own religious beliefs. Yet it is unclear what
this means for the evolution-creationism controversy. Does
teaching creationism rather than evolution constitute a breach of
the First Amendment? And isn't the teaching of biblical creationism, even alongside evolution, an endorsement of fundamental-
ist Christianity? Why not teach Hopi creationism or any of a
thousand other religious accounts of creation? If only one text is
presented (the Bible), the implication is that it, and no other, is
sacred. Likewise, does teaching evolution rather than creationism constitute a constraint on freedom of expression?

Many are upset by what they see as the intrusion of theological
ideas into the scientific curriculum. Science and science education organizations, in particular, are concerned. The National

Association of Biology Teachers, the National Center for Science Education, and the National Science Teachers Association have all issued statements urging that evolution alone should be taught in America's schools. They worry that the decisions to restrict the teaching of evolution politicize science and that students in states like Kansas and Georgia will be unprepared for standardized tests like the SAT and for scientific fields like medicine and biology. Furthermore, students must be able to critically assess whether creationism is true, and they can do this only with a full and careful understanding of the evolutionary account of life's origins.

For others, though, it is wrong to teach only evolution—this constitutes discrimination against competing theories of life's origins. If you describe evolution as merely a theory, not fact, you open the door to religious viewpoints. For example, the Cobb County Board of Education claims that its policy, which allows the teaching of evolution and creationism, embodies freedom of thought and religion: "The purpose of this policy is to foster critical thinking among students, to allow academic freedom consistent with legal requirements, to promote tolerance and acceptance of a diversity of opinion, and to ensure a posture of neutrality toward religion" (Cobb County Board of Education 2002).

Discussion Questions

1. Does teaching creationism rather than evolution constitute an unfair endorsement of one worldview?

2. Does teaching evolution and not creationism constitute a constraint on freedom of expression?

3. Should a public school offer a balanced curriculum, teaching both nonreligious and religious theories about the origins of life?

Resources

Center for Scientific Creation. 2003. www.creationscience.com/ (accessed October 4, 2003).

Cobb County Board of Education. 2002. "Policy on Theories of Origin." www.cobb.k12.ga.us/news/originpolicy.htm (accessed October 4, 2003).

DAWKINS, RICHARD. 1996. *Climbing Mount Improbable*. New York: W. W. Norton.

Epperson v. Arkansas, 393 U.S. 97 (1968).

Exploring Constitutional Conflicts. "Evolution/Creation," www.law.umkc.edu/faculty/projects/ftrials/conlaw/evolution.htm (accessed October 4, 2003).

LERNER, LAWRENCE. 2000. *Good Science, Bad Science: Teaching Evolution in the States*. Dayton, OH: Fordham Foundation Report.

MONTAGU, ASHLEY, ed. 1984. *Science and Creationism*. New York: Oxford University Press.

National Academy of Sciences. 1998. *Teaching about Evolution and the Nature of Science*. Washington, DC: National Academy Press.

CREATIONISM, TAKE TWO: PROFESSOR DINI'S RECOMMENDATION

Michael Dini, an associate professor of biology at Texas Tech University, has been at the center of a recent creationism-evolution controversy. If you visit the Web site of Professor Dini at Texas Tech University, you will find the following text:

> If you set up an appointment to discuss the writing of a letter of recommendation, I will ask you: "How do you account for the scientific origin of the human species?" If you will not give a scientific answer to this question, then you should not seek my recommendation.
>
> Why do I ask this question? Let's consider the situation of one wishing to enter medical school. Whereas medicine is

historically rooted first in the practice of magic and later in religion, modern medicine is an endeavor that springs from the sciences, biology prominent among these. The central, unifying principle of biology is the theory of evolution, which includes both micro- and macro-evolution, and which extends to ALL species. Someone who ignores the most important theory in biology cannot expect to properly practice in a field that is now so heavily based on biology. . . .

Good medicine, like good biology, is based on the collection and evaluation of physical evidence. So much physical evidence supports the evolution of humans from non-human ancestors that one can validly refer to the "fact" of human evolution, even if all of the details are not yet known; just as one can refer to the "fact" of gravity, even if all of the details of gravitational theory are not yet known. One can ignore this evidence only at the risk of calling into question one's understanding of science and the scientific method. Scientists do not ignore logical conclusions based on abundant scientific evidence and experimentation because these conclusions do not conform to expectations or beliefs.

— (www2tltc.ttu.edu/ dini/Personal/letters.htm)

According to Dini, he is not forcing students to hold a certain viewpoint; he is simply requiring science students to be scientific. He says he cannot, in good conscience, recommend a student for graduate study in biology if that student does not accept the theory of evolution. Evolution is not a matter of personal opinion; it is a fact of science, according to Dini.

Dini is being accused of religious discrimination and is being investigated by the Justice Department because a student, Micah Spradley, filed a legal complaint against him. Critics of Dini argue that he is acting unfairly. The basis for writing student recommendations should be the quality of the students' work, not the particulars of their personal belief system. Texas Tech has thus far stood behind Professor Dini. The chancellor released a letter in which he noted that there are 38 other faculty members who can write recommendations for science students.

Discussion Questions

1. What are the strengths and weaknesses of Dini's arguments?

2. Is Dini being unfair to students?

3. Could a creationist be a top-notch scientist? A biologist?

4. Would you trust a creationist to be your doctor?

5. Does Dini appear to be going out of his way to make a point, by posting his recommendation policies on his Web site instead of talking to individual students in private? And, if so, is there anything wrong with this?

Resources

Dini's Web site. www2.tltc.ttu.edu/dini/ (accessed October 4, 2003).
MADIGAN, NICK. 2003. "Professor's Snub of Creationists Prompts U.S. Inquiry." *New York Times*, February 2.

SPORTS SUPPLEMENTATION: FAIR OR FOUL?

Athletes have myriad ways to enhance their performance. They use intricately designed training programs, hire expensive coaches, and buy specialized equipment. They adhere to strict and sometimes bizarre diets, and they load up on caffeine and electrolytes, salt and potassium. They use amphetamines to decrease reaction time and anabolic steroids to build muscle mass and take injections of the hormone erythropoietin to stimulate overproduction of red blood cells and thus increase their body's oxygen-carrying capacity. Soon there may be technology that allows the insertion of synthetic muscle-enhancing genes—for example, the so-called the IGF-1 gene—to make muscles stronger, less prone to damage, and quicker. Are all of these modes of enhancement ethically equivalent? And, if not, why not?

There seems to be consensus among athletes, sports organizations, and spectators that certain kinds of performance enhancement are unfair. For example, the evidence that a number of top athletes including Marion Jones, Jason Giambi, and Dwain Chambers were using tetrahydrogestrinone (THG), a "designer steroid," during competition set off a scandal—yet another in a long string of scandals in athletics over the past several decades. But why? Enhancing performance is as old as athletic competition itself. Why are Dwain Chambers's anabolic steroids unfair, while Lance Armstrong's state-of-the-art (and very expensive) bicycle frame, wheels, rims, helmet, and tires are just impressive?

Over the past several decades, the practice of doping (ingesting foreign substances for enhanced competition) has become the hallmark of unfair enhancement. Restrictions of the use of drugs during competition arose in the 1920s, and regular testing of athletes began in the 1950s when evidence emerged of drug use in several European cycling and track races. Since then, testing has become a routine part of high-level competition. After a doping scandal rocked the Tour de France in 1999, the World Anti-Doping Agency (WADA) was set up to oversee anti-doping policies and testing strategies internationally. It aims to "protect the *Athletes'* fundamental right to participate in doping-free sport and thus promote health, fairness, and equality for *Athletes* worldwide" (World Anti-Doping Agency 2003). The spirit of sport is characterized, according to the WADA, by certain values. These values include health, fair play, excellence in performance, fun and joy, teamwork, courage, respect for rules and laws, and respect for self and other participants. Doping is contrary to this spirit of playing fair.

Substances prohibited in competition by the WADA include various stimulants, narcotics (e.g., morphine and oxycodone),

cannabinoids, anabolic steroids, peptide hormones, beta-2 ago-
nists, blood doping, and gene doping.

Perhaps the difference between doping and enhancements
like a fancy bike comes down to what might be called trans-
parency. Equipment, training, coaching—these are done openly.
Drug use is usually secretive. Athletes are proud of their bikes
and rackets and goggles—and no one looks askance at these
enhancements. But doping with drugs is typically done on the sly,
and athletes who are "exposed" are often ridiculed and shamed
by the media. They are less than excellent athletes because they
have cheated.

Some distinguish between drugs used for training enhancement and those used for performance enhancement. The argument is that there is nothing wrong with taking a drug that
increases your capacity to train hard—even anabolic steroids.
While training, you are competing only against yourself, creating
a body that is faster, stronger, more agile than your competitor's.
However, taking a drug for competition is unfair because it offers
an advantage.

If doping in sport were legal and everyone could do it, would
it still be unfair? Everyone would have the same advantage,
assuming everyone took the same enhancement drugs. Yet there
is something contrived about this. Part of the spirit of sport is to
compare people's natural abilities. Furthermore, many of the
enhancing drugs are harmful to those who take them, so coerc-
ing athletes to dope simply to remain competitive would obviously be bad for sports. Some believe that doping among athletes
is so widespread that this subtle coercion into a culture of doping
has already occurred.

A number of ethical problems also plague the current practice of testing athletes for drug use. There is controversy over
which drugs should be banned and which not. Some testing is
involuntary and may constitute an invasion of privacy. And
some tests, such as blood draws, are invasive enough to pose ethical problems when mandatory. Some argue that invasive testing
can be justified only if there is a threat of harm to third persons.
So, what are the potential harms to others? That the athlete will
unfairly compete with opponents? That the sports community

will somehow be damaged? That young people often idolize athletes and drug use will set a bad example?

Discussion Questions

1. Should drug use be banned from athletic competition? Why or why not?

2. Is there a sharp line between natural and artificial methods of enhancement?

3. Are all artificial enhancements unfair?

4. What constitutes fair competition?

5. Tiger Woods allegedly had Lasik eye surgery to achieve better than normal eyesight. Is this fair play?

Resources

DREW, CHRISTOPHER. 2003. "Complaints and Support for Diet Pill at Congressional Hearing." *New York Times*, July 24, A12.

DREW, CHRISTOPHER. 2003. "Official Urges Ban of Ephedra by Baseball." *New York Times*, July 25, C19.

MCNEIL, DONALD G. 2003. "Acting Quickly, U.S. Bans Newfound Steroid." *New York Times*, October 29, C17.

The President's Council on Bioethics. 2003. "Beyond Therapy: Biotechnology and the Pursuit of Happiness." www.bioethics.gov/reports/ beyondtherapy.html (accessed November 24, 2003).

United States Anti-Doping Agency. 2003. "A Brief History of Anti-Doping." www.usantidoping.org/ (accessed January 6, 2004).

WILSON, WAYNE, and EDWARD DERSE, eds. 2001. *Doping in Elite Sport.* Champaign, IL: Human Kinetics.

World Anti-Doping Agency. 2003. *The World Anti-Doping Code.* www.wada-ama.org/docs/web/standards_harmonization/code/list_standard_2004.pdf (accessed June 8, 2004).

SPORTS SUPPLEMENTATION, TAKE TWO: ROSS REBAGLIATI

In 1998, Ross Rebagliati was stripped of his Olympic gold medal in snowboarding because he tested positive for marijuana. Marijuana does not improve performance and, if anything, is probably detrimental to performance. Many fans and fellow athletes considered his punishment unfair. Rebagliati had broken Olympic rules, which forbid ingesting pot, but he hadn't cheated; smoking the marijuana had given him no competitive advantage.

Discussion Questions

1. Should Ross Rebagliati have been stripped of his gold medal?

2. If marijuana offers no advantage to athletes, what might be the justification for making its use against the rules?

3. Is random drug testing of athletes an unjustified invasion of their privacy?

EXTREME MAKEOVER

Biological fate doesn't just give us disabilities and disorders. To a large degree, it gives us who we are. Our bodies are us. Yet our inner selves do not always match our physical forms. Our bodies impose definitions and limitations that falsify our identities and frustrate our purposes.

— Virginia Postrel (2003)

ABC has been brilliantly successful with its reality show called *Extreme Makeover*. Each Wednesday night, viewers watch two or three lucky people undergo a physical transformation. The plot is simple: take an ugly person and make him or her, well, less ugly—perhaps, in some cases, even attractive.

Viewers see the contestants first in their home environment, with special emphasis on the hardships of being unattractive—catcalls from cars driving by, lack of self-esteem, a lifelong wish to for once feel like a princess or a prince. Then they get the surprise knock on the door from *Extreme Makeover*—yes, you have been chosen! There are tears and hugs, smiles, and a bit of trepidation. They are about to undergo a radical and painful transformation. They may not even recognize themselves afterward.

The contestants travel to Hollywood, where they will spend, on average, about three to six months being cut and reconfigured by the country's most exclusive plastic surgeons. We are privy to their first meeting with the surgeon, who asks them what it is about their face that they would like to change, and offers suggestions. "Your nose is too long; a stronger chin would give you a more classic look; your eyes droop down at the edges and are too puffy. . . ." Then on to the body: breasts are too small and a bit saggy; and always there is more fat around the belly and on the thighs than desired. And so it goes. An ideal of beauty—Hollywood style—serves as template for reconfiguring face and body.

Part of the appeal of *Extreme Makeover* is its gruesome attention to the pain of plastic surgery. We see oblique shots of the surgeon, hard at work over a face or a stomach; a needle injecting saline into a breast implant; a very large hypodermic needle sucking out clots of yellow fat during liposuction. The patient is filmed shortly after surgery, bandaged and swollen, looking far more grotesque than before.

After the cutting and some initial healing, the participants move on to somewhat more superficial changes: They see a cosmetic dentist, who bleaches their teeth or puts on porcelain veneers. They spend a couple weeks working with a personal trainer, to firm and tone. Finally they get a visit from Sam, the fashion man, who will overhaul their wardrobes and help them pick something absolutely stunning for their "reveal"—the culmination of the show, where the participants reemerge into the world of their friends and family.

The popularity of *Extreme Makeover* may reflect a growing interest in, and acceptance of, plastic surgery as a way to alter one's physical appearance. According to the American Society of Plastic Surgeons, more than 2 million people had cosmetic plastic surgery in 2002, nearly triple the number a decade ago. Eighty-five percent of plastic surgery patients are women, and those between 35 and 50 were the most likely to have a procedure done.

Botox—an injection of botulinum toxin that reduces the appearance of wrinkles by relaxing muscle cells—is by far the most popular plastic surgery procedure: More than a million people have Botox injections every year. Among the other cosmetic plastic surgery procedures available are tummy tuck, breast enlargement or reduction, breast lift, chemical peel with phenol and trichloroacetic acid, collagen injections, dermabrasion, eyelid surgery, facelift, facial implants, forehead lift, hair replacement surgery, laser facial resurfacing, liposuction, and nose surgery.

For *Extreme Makeover* participants, the bill is footed by ABC. But many other people will spend thousands of dollars for cosmetic procedures. One Botox injection costs, on average, just under $400. Liposuction costs about $2,000, breast augmentation will run you about $3,000 (with another $2,000 if you decide to have the implants removed), a tummy tuck about $4,000, and a facelift about $5,000. Total expenditures on cosmetic surgery procedures in the United States for 2001 totaled about $6.9 billion. Cosmetic plastic surgery (as opposed to reconstructive plastic surgery) is usually considered elective by health insurance plans and is not covered.

Discussion Questions

1. Does *Extreme Makeover* exploit its participants?

2. Is there anything wrong with surgically modifying our bodies or faces?

3. In light of the prevalence of social ills such as hunger and poverty, is there anything morally wrong with an individual spending a couple of thousand dollars on liposuction or breast implants?

Resources

American Society of Plastic Surgeons. 2003. "Cosmetic Plastic Surgery Procedures at a Glance." http://plasticsurgery.org/public_education/procedures/CosmeticPlasticSurgery.cfm (accessed November 22, 2003).

ELLIOTT, CARL. 2003. *Better Than Well: American Medicine Meets the American Dream.* New York: W. W. Norton.

HAIKEN, ELIZABETH. 1997. *Venus Envy: A History of Cosmetic Surgery.* Baltimore, MD: Johns Hopkins University Press,

KRON, JOAN. 1998. *Lift: Wanting, Fearing—and Having—A Face-Lift.* New York: Viking.

POSTREL, VIRGINIA. 2003. "Going to Great Lengths." *New York Times Magazine,* August 31, 16.

CULTURE WARS

The phrase "culture wars" has been used to describe the increasingly polarized nature of public discourse in America. The debate has turned vitriolic on certain key issues such as homosexuality, abortion, and education. Two strongly conflicting camps seem to be separated not merely by political agenda but by radically different moral worldviews.

In 1991, sociologist James Davison Hunter published a book called *Culture Wars*, in which he tries to understand why the cultural conflict over certain issues is so bitter and unrelenting. The conflict is a hostile one, he says, because the end point is the domination of one system of moral belief, one ethos, over another, each of which provides a sense of identity, community, and national purpose. These moral differences are expressed as "polarizing tendencies": the impulse toward orthodoxy and the impulse toward progressivism.

As Hunter defines it, orthodoxy is characterized by the belief that moral values are based in some notion of an external, transcendent authority. As such, moral values are universal and timeless. Moral truth is revealed in the Bible, and this should be our source for moral guidance. The orthodox impulse is perhaps most obviously present in the worldviews of people with strong faith commitments, who consider God, Yahweh, or Allah the source of moral law. Nevertheless, even some secular humanists tend toward orthodoxy: instead of God, nature may serve as an external and clearly defining authority for the moral life.

For progressives, moral values have no ultimate or timeless foundation; rather, morality is an expression and extension of human rationality. We discover, even create, values as society evolves and in response to the challenges and needs of society. Truth "tends to be viewed as a process, a reality ever unfolding" (Hunter 1991, p. 44). Those progressivists who identify with a particular religious tradition interpret scripture in light of progressivist assumptions. For example, they reject biblical literalism in favor of a more individualistic faith whereby each person interprets the scripture for himself or herself. They will be more inclined to derive broad values from scripture, such as "be compassionate," than from specific rules. A large number of progressivists are secular—that is, they hold to no particular religious affiliation and may consider themselves agnostic or atheistic. They may nevertheless have deep humanistic concern for the welfare of other people and are often actively involved in causes like environmental conservation, international justice, and social equality.

Although Hunter is careful not to equate orthodoxy and progressivism with political parties, he does argue that there is a strong correlation of orthodoxy with conservative politics and progressivism with a liberal or libertarian social agenda. Controversies over gay marriage, prayer in school, abortion, the right to die, and other key dividing issues constitute the political battleground of the culture wars. These political debates are an expression of a cultural conflict, and they trace back to the bitter disagreement over basic moral vision. This is why compromise, the hallmark of political debate in a democracy, is so elusive in the battle over these issues: When it comes down to matters of ultimate moral truth, one cannot compromise.

Discussion Questions

1. What is the ultimate source of moral authority?

2. Describe the kind of dialogue characteristic of a conflict of worldviews.

3. Is Hunter right about these polarizing tendencies?

4. Do you tend toward the progressivist or the orthodox worldview? Why?

5. In what other cases in this book are the "culture wars" most evident?

Resources

American Family Association. 2003. "No Gay Marriage." www.nogaymarriage.com (accessed June 8, 2004).

HUNTER, JAMES DAVISON. 1991. *Culture Wars: The Struggle to Define America*. New York: Basic Books.
BENNETT, WILLIAM J. 1994. *The De-valuing of America*. Focus on the Family Publishing.
Christian Coalition of America. www.cc.org (accessed January 4, 2004).

BRIGHT RIGHTS

If you are one of those people who don't believe in God, you may be feeling a bit downtrodden these days. If so, you can join a growing number of like-minded individuals who want to proclaim their beliefs without shame or embarrassment. You can join the Brights, an international Internet constituency of like-minded people. Through cyberspace, the Brights hope to influence political and social culture. Brights are people whose worldview is naturalistic, devoid of any mystical or supernatural elements. Brights don't believe in ghosts, aliens, miracles, astrology, or God. Calling all skeptics, atheists, agnostics, humanists, secularists, nontheists, and freethinkers.

The Brights are sick of being the silent majority. In America, it is not a nice thing to be called godless. It is politically correct to be tolerant of other viewpoints—but somehow this tolerance has not extended to the atheists among us. But why, the Brights ask, should this be so? Rationalism or a purely scientific worldview is more defensible than one that revolves around a deity. The Brights, just as well as anyone else, can live principled lives that contribute to the civic order and the global community.

Our public culture is becoming more aggressively religious. Atheistic and secular humanistic beliefs are increasingly marginalized. President Bush regularly invokes God, and the Bush administration has tried to increase the role of religion in public life. Candidates for public office must be good churchgoers. They may be female, African American, even gay. But God forbid that they be atheist, at least openly.

This, say the Brights, is just not right. The United States is founded on the idea of freedom of thought—the freedom not only to practice whatever religion you want but also to practice no religion at all. Although the Brights remain quiet, for fear of being disparaged or disliked, there are many among us. According to a survey by the Pew Forum on Religion and Public Life, 27 million Americans identify themselves as atheist, agnostic, or having no religious affiliation. This is roughly 10 percent of the population—a healthy minority. The Brights are particularly well-represented among scientists (93 percent of scientists who belong to the National Academy of Sciences would be considered Brights, according to a 1996 study).

Discussion Questions

1. How would you answer some of the questions Brights ask?

    a. Would you vote for an otherwise qualified candidate for public office who was a Bright?

    b. Would you support a nominee for the Supreme Court who was a Bright?

    c. Should Brights be allowed to teach high school?

2. Does a religious worldview provide a better foundation for morality than a secular worldview does? Or vice versa?

3. Are the Brights correct in saying that there is discrimination against atheists in American culture?

Resources

The Brights' Net. www.the-brights.net.
DENNETT, DANIEL C. 2003. "The Bright Stuff." *New York Times*, July 12. Also available at http://the-brights.net/dennett_nyt.htm.
SHERMER, MICHAEL. 2003. "The Big 'Bright' Brouhaha." *The Skeptic*. www.skeptic.com/BIG%20BRIGHT%20BROUHAHA4.htm (accessed January 4, 2004).

A CALL TO CIVIL SOCIETY

On May 27, 1998, the Council on Civil Society, a nonpartisan group of scholars and leaders, released its report, *A Call to Civil Society: Why Democracy Needs Moral Truths*.

America's civic institutions are declining because the moral ideas that fueled and formed them are losing their power—the power to shape our behavior, to unite us as one people in pursuit of common ideals.

Too many Americans view morality as a threat to freedom, rather than its essential guarantor. The deeper solution, the Council concludes, is to recover the ideas that moral truth exists and that democracy depends upon certain moral truths. Democracy embodies the truth that all persons possess equal dignity.

Hence, the Council concludes that the nation's main challenge at the close of the century is to rediscover the existence of transmittable moral truth and to strengthen the moral habits and ways of living that make democracy possible.

Discussion Questions

1. What are America's civic institutions?

2. What are the moral ideals that formed and fueled America's civic institutions?

3. Is the power of these institutions threatened? Is this a good or bad thing?

4. In what ways might morality be a threat to freedom?

5. How might we strengthen moral habits?

Resources

Council on Civil Society. 1998. *A Call to Civil Society: Why Democracy Needs Moral Truths*. Chicago: Council on Civil Society.

ETHICS FOR THE INFORMATION AGE: THE SCANS REPORT

In 1991, the U.S. Department of Labor published a report outlining the various skills children should be taught in order to achieve a high-performing and technologically proficient workforce.

> The Secretary's Commission on Achieving Necessary Skills (SCANS) was appointed by the Secretary of Labor to determine the skills our young people need to succeed in the world of work. The Commission's fundamental purpose is to encourage a high-performance economy characterized by high-skill, high-wage employment.

In addition to basic skills such as writing and reading, and thinking skills such as problem solving and decision making, the secretary of labor determined that children need to learn a particular set of moral skills (what the report calls personal skills). These skills are as follows (verbatim from the report):

Responsibility

Exerts a high level of effort and perseverance towards goal attainment. Works hard to become excellent at doing tasks by setting high standards, paying attention to details, working well, and displaying a high level concentration even when assigned an unpleasant task. Displays high standards of attendance, punctuality, enthusiasm, vitality, and optimism in approaching and completing tasks.

Self-Esteem

Believes in own self-worth and maintains a positive view of self; demonstrates knowledge of own skills and abilities; is aware of impact on others; and knows own emotional capacity and needs and how to address them.

Sociability

Demonstrates understanding, friendliness, adaptability, empathy, and politeness in new and ongoing group settings. Asserts self in familiar and unfamiliar social situations; relates well to others; responds appropriately as the situation requires; and takes an interest in what others say and do.

Self-Management

Assesses own knowledge, skills, and abilities accurately; sets well-defined and realistic personal goals; monitors progress toward goal attainment and motivates self through goal achievement; exhibits self-control and responds to feedback unemotionally and nondefensively; is a "self-starter."

Integrity/Honesty

Can be trusted. Recognizes when faced with making a decision or exhibiting behavior that may break with commonly-held personal or societal values; understands the impact of violating these beliefs and codes on an organization, self, and others; and chooses an ethical course of action.

Discussion Questions

1. Is there anything controversial about this list of values?

2. What values are missing, if any?

3. Should it be the goal of public schools to produce an efficient workforce? Are there other competing goals?

Resources

U.S. Department of Labor. 1991. *What Work Requires of Schools: A SCANS Report for America 2000.* The Secretary's Commission on Achieving Necessary Skills.

CHARACTER EDUCATION OF CHILDREN

Over the last decade years, schools in almost every state have introduced character education programs. Many schools, school districts, and states now *require* some form of character education in the schools. The Department of Education has given $27 million in character education grants since 1995. So, just what is character education, and why has it become so popular in the last few years?

Character, or values, education is designed to teach children to become honest, responsible, engaged citizens. Dr. Thomas Lickona, a professor of education and spokesperson for the Character Education Network, defines character education as "the deliberate effort to develop virtues that are good for the individual and good for society." The "objective goodness of virtues" can be tested by seeing whether they affirm human dignity, promote individual well-being and the common good, define human rights and obligations, and "meet the classical ethical tests of reversibility (Would you want to be treated this way?) and universalizability (Would you want all persons to act this way in a similar situation?)" (Character Education Network 2003).

Character education is not a new phenomenon. Indeed, character education was for hundreds of years seen as the primary function of educational institutions. This began to change in the 1960s, and for several decades teachers functioned mainly to impart academic knowledge; the teaching of values, it was thought, should be left to parents or clergy. Now the tide seems to be turning again, toward an integration of character education into the larger educational agenda.

Several trends have contributed to the revival of interest in character. First, scientific research on the development of morals in children increasingly suggests that morality does not just arise unbidden from the soul, but must be nurtured. Although all people may be born with the capacity to be moral, character needs to be shaped in the right directions. As more is understood about how moral sensibility is developed, there is a heightened sense that morality can and should be actively *taught*, not only by parents, but through schools and organizations as well.

There is also a feeling among many that the moral foundations of America have been corroding for some time now. Not only is there an epidemic of immoral behavior among adults (divorce, adultery, business scandals), but children are showing signs of moral trouble, too: they take drugs, have sex, bully one another, and cheat in school. The Josephson Institute of Ethics, for example, polled 12,000 high school students in 1998: 74 percent admitted to cheating on a test. Parents do not seem to be doing enough to cultivate good character, so it is important that schools step in and fill the gap.

Different educators and researchers argue for the superiority of one or another approach to character education, but the fact is, no one really knows what works best. Some favor the "inculcation" approach: the student needs to accept the norms of society. Behind this is the assumption that the needs of society transcend and define the needs and goals of the individual (William Bennett, former secretary of education, holds this view). Others favor the "critical thinking" approach, in which you teach children to use logic and reason to analyze moral problems and make decisions on their own. The assumption here is that students have their own unique set of values, which we should respect; our goal is to help them clarify their own views. Still others see morality as a series of stages of development (à la developmental psychologist Lawrence Kohlberg) and approach character education as the process of helping students work through the various stages.

Those teaching character education have to decide what good character is and how it is formed, measured, and taught. Each of these aspects is controversial and marks an uncomfortable intersection between science and values. Moreover, the influences on moral development are varied: genetics, parents, peers, modeling by other adults, institutions (churches, scouting troops, and so on), media (the influences of television, music, and video), and school.

One of the bugaboos of character education is the politically charged question of whether education should be "values neutral" or "normative." If we argue for a normative approach, then which values—and whose values—do we teach? Are there core values on which we can all agree? Below are the lists of values or character traits that children should be taught, according to various educational organizations.

The U.S. Department of Labor's Secretary's Commission on Achieving Necessary Skills (SCANS) report:

responsibility
self-esteem
sociability
self-management
honesty/integrity

The Josephson Institute for Ethics:

respect
responsibility
trustworthiness
caring

justice and fairness
civic virtue and citizenship

The Council for Global Education (these are values implied or stated in the Constitution and the Bill of Rights):

compassion	order
courtesy	objectivity
critical inquiry	participation
due process	rational consent
equality of opportunity	reasoned argument
freedom of thought and action	respect for others' rights
human worth and dignity	responsible citizenship
integrity	responsibility
justice	rule of law
knowledge	tolerance
loyalty	truth

The Character Education Network:

responsibility
perseverance
caring
self-discipline
citizenship
honesty
courage
fairness
respect

Not surprisingly, many are critical of character education programs in public schools. Some argue than morality is far more complicated than a set of character traits such as honesty. You cannot teach a student to make nuanced choices by teaching them a set of abstract principles like "be truthful." Simply following rules is not enough because sometimes acting morally requires going against a rule. Even deception can be the right thing to do. The hard part is being able to make critical and reflective judgments about moral problems. Others are bothered by the idea of public schools taking on the job of shaping public morality because the values endorsed by the government are not shared by all of its citizens.

Discussion Questions

1. Is there much difference in the lists of values promoted by various institutions and groups?

2. Should these values be taught in schools?

3. How do you think moral character is developed in an individual?

Resources

BENNETT, WILLIAM J. 1993. *The Book of Virtues.* New York: Simon & Schuster.

Character Education Network. 2003. "What Is Character Education?" www.charactered.net/main/traits.asp (accessed November 30, 2003).

GILBERT, SUSAN. 2003. "Scientists Explore the Molding of Children's Morals." *New York Times*, March 16, D5.

HUITT, WILLIAM. 2000. "Moral and Character Development." Educational Psychology Interactive. http://chiron.valdosta.edu/whuitt/col/morchr/morchr.html (accessed December 1, 2003).

The Josephson Institute of Ethics. www.josephsoninstitute.org/ (accessed January 14, 2004).

KAGAN, JEROME, and SHARON LAMB, eds. 1987. *The Emergence of Morality in Young Children.* Chicago: University of Chicago Press.

NUCCI, LARRY P. 2001. *Education in the Moral Domain.* Cambridge: Cambridge University Press.

PUTNAM, ROBERT D. 2000. *Bowling Alone.* New York: Simon & Schuster.

TURIEL, ELLIOT. 2002. *The Culture of Morality.* Cambridge: Cambridge University Press.

CHARACTER EDUCATION, TAKE TWO: GEORGIA'S "RESPECT FOR THE CREATOR" PRINCIPLE

An August 1997 statute added to the Official Code of Georgia (Section 20-2-145) requires the State Board of Education to develop a comprehensive character education program. As explained in the Board of Education's policy statement, *Values and Character Education Implementation Guide,* children from kindergarten to grade twelve will be encouraged to develop 41 character traits, including civility, compassion, courtesy, honesty, patience, diligence, frugality, moderation, cleanliness, punctuality, democracy, courage, loyalty, and tolerance. Nestled among the other values—number 31 in the alphabetical listing—is "respect for the creator." Unlike the other 40 values, which are given only a few words' explanation, number 31 receives a full paragraph of explanation and defense.

The commentary is by Georgia's Attorney General Thurbert E. Baker:

> Our most basic freedoms and rights are not granted to us from the government but they are intrinsically ours. . . . This is to say that the founders of the republic recognized a higher authority, a power greater than themselves that endowed every human being with certain unalienable rights. . . . In the Declaration of Independence, Thomas Jefferson names this life force that permeates the universe and from which our unalienable rights stem the "creator". . . . This cannot be interpreted as a promotion of religion or even as a promotion of the belief in a personal God, but only as an acknowledgement that the intrinsic worth of every individual derives from no government, person or group of persons, but is something that each of us is born with. . . .

Discussion Questions

1. Is "respect for the creator" an appropriate value for a public school to require as part of its character curriculum?

2. Assess Baker's defense of the "respect for creator" value. What are the strengths and weaknesses of his argument?

Resources

Georgia Department of Education. 1997. *Values and Character Education Implementation Guide.* Office of Policy and Communications, August.

RIGOBERTA MENCHÚ: THE PURPOSE OF TRUTH

In 1983, a book titled *I, Rigoberta Menchú: An Indian Woman in Guatemala* was published and gained popularity around the world. The book is a memoir about Menchú's life as a Quiché Indian in Guatemala. As Menchú says, it is not just her own story but the story of "all poor Guatemalans." "My personal experience is the reality of a whole people." She describes in vivid detail the customs and rituals surrounding birth, marriage, and death of the Quiché, one of 22 indigenous ethnic groups in Guatemala. She also recounts the discrimination against indigenous Indians during the country's bitter civil conflict.

In 1999, anthropologist David Stoll published a book in which he challenged the veracity of Menchú's story. He claimed that she had altered key details and had recounted events that she could not have witnessed. The implication was that Menchú had lied, blending her story with the larger story of Indians in Guatemala, in order to further her cause as a guerilla organizer. Stoll's book was widely reported in the media, and it led many to feel let down by Menchú and to question the value of her book.

Supporters of Menchú argued that whether or not every detail in the book is true matters little. First of all, Menchú did (accurately) describe her story as the story of all poor Guatemalans. Furthermore, whether or not every detail is true is less important than the larger truth about repression and human rights violations. The fact remains that her book raised global awareness about profound human rights violations in Guatemala.

Discussion Questions

1. Does the veracity of Menchu's story matter more than its impact?

2. How would one define "truth" in this case?

Resources

ARIAS, ARTURO, ed. 2001. *The Rigoberta Menchú Controversy.* Minneapolis: University of Minnesota Press.

MENCHÚ, RIGOBERTA. 1983. *I, Rigoberta Menchú: An Indian Woman in Guatemala.* Edited and introduced by Elisabeth Burgos-Debray. Translated by Ann Wright. New York: Verso.

STOLL, DAVID. 1999. *Rigoberta Menchú and the Story of All Poor Guatemalans.* Boulder, CO: Westview Press.